hanging on by a

Thread

Dr. Walter S. Thomas, Sr.

DEDICATION

· ·

I want to dedicate this work to my family, led by my wonderful wife and soulmate, Patricia, and our children and their families. Also, special thanks to the New Psalmist Baptist Church, a people I love so dearly, for being the laboratory where I have the opportunity to test my theories, hone my skills, and still be privileged to be called their pastor. I thank my God every day for the life I am so blessed to live.

5/18/17
05:04 IG
04:25 OUT

Hanging On By a Thread
by Dr. Walter S. Thomas, Sr.

For information, address:

The Church Online, LLC
1000 Ardmore Blvd.
Pittsburgh, PA 15221

International Standard Book Number: 978-1-940786-45-2

Library of Congress Catalogue Card Number: Available Upon Request

Printed in the United States of America

First Edition, January, 2017

Trademarks

Bishop Walter Scott Thomas brings a wealth of his life's experience to a broad audience that is sure to provoke thought and self-examination for those who are serious about dealing with the pressures of everyday life and work. This book is a must-read as Bishop Thomas lays out strategies to help clarify goals, objectives, and priorities that minimize the stress of leadership in every arena of life.

Rev. Dwight S. Riddick, Sr. D. Min
Gethsemane Baptist Church
Newport News, VA

• •

Bishop Walter Scott Thomas has the audacity to tackle the mysterious and unspoken misnomers of management and the challenge of maintaining balance both personally and professionally. Life throws curveballs to the least and greatest and crisis (crises) can't always be calculated. When life happens, we'll need a template to help us navigate the course. Here it is!

Dr. Anthony Michael Chandler, Sr.
Cedar Street Baptist Church
Richmond, VA

• •

One of the most consistent and powerful voices in this era has been the voice of Dr. Walter S. Thomas. In this book he gives us necessary tips on how to handle the pressure of being responsible with the privilege of leadership. Thank you, Dr. Thomas, for hearing the cries of the leader and answering the voice that is sometimes silenced by the pressure.

Dr. Dwayne C. Debnam
Morning Star Baptist Church
Baltimore, MD

In this must-read account, Dr. Walter S. Thomas is the epitome of our 21st century scholar and a realist of our time. He communicates how becoming in touch with our psyche and challenging situations in life will allow us to progress and maintain true sanity without having to prove to the world that we are perfect or can't handle true pressure. Dr. Thomas elucidates the dynamics of critical thinking in his book and leads us to the pathway of balance in life applications.

Bishop Eric D. Garnes, D. Min, MPS
Tabernacle of Praise
Brooklyn, New York

. . . .

We live in a cultural climate where overexertion, overextension, and over-commitment have become social norms. It is as if self-destructive tendencies and living with an unsustainable pace has become an admirable badge of success. With clarity and candor, Dr. Walter Thomas eloquently and passionately refutes this notion. He masterfully articulates the importance of stewarding your most important asset: you. This book is a must-read for anyone who is more concerned with who they are, opposed to what they do. If I can use biblical imagery I would simply say, allow this book to teach you to have a Mary heart in a Martha world.

Dr. Dharius Daniels
Kingdom Church Ewing, NJ
Author, RePresent Jesus

TABLE OF CONTENTS

· ·

FOREWORD

· · · · · · · · · · · · · · · · · ·

From Dr. William H. Curtis
Senior Pastor, Mount Ararat
Baptist Church

Growing up in church is always a privilege. Growing up in New Psalmist Baptist Church and receiving Bishop Walter Thomas as my Spiritual Father was a downright blessing hand-delivered from God, an incomparable gift. From the moment I met him, he took me in, training and strengthening me and stretching my faith in God. His wisdom only encouraged me in my calling, pushing me to be the man of God I am today. It is a true pleasure to serve as his son in ministry.

From initial sermon to the Presidency of the Hampton University Minister's Conference, Bishop Thomas has inspired and mentored me to accept assignments that required total surrender to God and an ever-increasing devotional life. I can still see him seated quietly in his chair in what we affectionately call Old Psalmist, journaling his prayers and expressing his heart to the Lord. For more than 30 years it has reminded me of the highest calling in a preacher's life, and that is to be a Christian nurturing a growing intimacy with God.

When I learned that Bishop Thomas was writing another book, I was ecstatic. As a Pastor, Certified Executive Coach, leader, friend, and proclaimed family man, he writes with conviction on a topic close to his heart. With shocking, brutal honesty, he challenges his own faith and questions the very idea of success itself. Letting words bleed onto the page like inspiration pouring from his lips, his unique combination of sage advice, professional experience, and psychological background will challenge the very way you live your life day-to-day.

The epitome of success, Bishop Thomas offers a unique perspective on the duality of life: the struggle of balancing a professional life with a personal one. From stories of health scares and trying to juggle speaking engagements with being a father, to the dark moment when he questioned his true calling, we get an eye-opening look into the life and mind of Bishop Thomas—past struggles, insecurities, and all. He owns up to the challenges he has faced over the years with admirable honesty, depth, and perspective, inspiring you to re-invest in your faith and de-invest in your bad habits.

Bishop Thomas writes for anyone suffering in silence, anyone struggling to slow down and take a breath, anyone needing a wake-up call, and anyone simply in need of a few encouraging words. With real-life examples as evidence, Bishop Thomas doesn't simply tell you to open up your eyes and take care of yourself. He takes it a step further by offering tried and true, step-by-step instructions and set principles. With candor, hope, and precision that will make you question yourself, his words force you to take a looking glass inside your mind to examine and understand the contents. Strengthening yourself and your faith, you'll no longer be hanging on by a thread.

Hanging On By a Thread is a tangible beacon of hope in an often tumultuous sea of accountability and expectations. So clear your schedule for the afternoon, settle in, turn the page, and renew your sense of faith. Who knows? Bishop Thomas' words may even inspire a pilgrimage of your own.

CHAPTER **ONE**

· ·

Nobody Really Knows You
(Until You Know Yourself)

*THIS IS A BOOK FOR LEADERS WHO ARE **HANGING ON BY A THREAD.***

When we started out as religious leaders, business leaders, and family leaders, it wasn't like that. We weren't so frayed apart and uncertain of ourselves. We knew who we were, what we wanted, and why we had chosen our paths. Yet, as we wake every morning to face the infinite, never-ending challenges arising in our daily lives, we find we just don't have the grasp on ourselves that we used to. We find the thread is fraying, and we're just barely hanging on.

Sure, we don't always show it. We have our duties planning sermons or business meetings, helping members of our congregations, or getting our kids off to school on time, as well as handling the administrative tasks of any modern life. Most of the time, we can handle these anticipated challenges without any sign of difficulty. We know what to expect from our roles in life, and we understand the responsibilities that we have to others. However, taking on the monumental task of trying to handle all of these different components is daunting. All it takes is one little extra challenge added to the mix, and we can quickly become completely overwhelmed, and worse, lost.

This is a book to help you find your way back, back to your drive, to your purpose, and most importantly, back to you. Though all people struggle with feelings of being lost and overwhelmed, those of us in positions of authority often struggle more than others. We often feel the need to remain strong and never let a crack show in our façade. We aren't allowed to show doubt, and we aren't allowed to be imperfect. Whenever we encounter a new challenge on top of those we deal with on a daily basis, we tend to handle it—as with everything else—on our own, never showing the stress that it creates or the angst and anger that it can sometimes cause. To do this, we often have to ignore our own needs so we can focus on the needs of those we are responsible for—a ministry, employees, or the little ones at home—leaving us to forge on alone, pushing through all of our problems and locking inside all the feelings that we should be disclosing.

This is a book to help you find your way back, back to your drive, to your purpose, and most importantly, back to you.

Normally, we can balance this, but we are always at risk of being blindsided by additional stresses and time-consuming tasks, which can push us over the edge. And in such situations, it is often those things we find most precious—our families, friends, and sense of self—that suffer and fall by the wayside. Handling the problems of others and making sure that our church, business, or family stays healthy and successful is undeniably fulfilling, but it can also stand to challenge our own personal well-being. We can end up losing sleep over the day-to-day business of our lives, giving up every bit of our own free time to take care of others and to solve problems. If we aren't able to find balance, this behavior will inevitably do us more harm than good. When we take the initiative to handle all these tasks on our own, instead of feeling fulfilled and in control, we often end up overwhelmed and stressed out. If we try to keep this pace up, we end up finding ourselves increasingly estranged from the person we thought we were. All of a sudden, we wake up and look in the mirror and discover, "Nobody knows me; nobody understands me. And I don't even know myself."

And that thread just gets thinner and thinner...

EVERYTHING TO EVERYONE, BUT NO ONE KNOWS YOU

I understand when people tell me that they feel no one knows them or understands their challenges. Many pastors feel that their role is to handle all the issues in the church and that they should not have to turn to others for advice or stress release. Outside the church, many managers and business owners feel they have to have all the answers and can't look to employees or others for direction. Parents have to run their families on their own, often fearing judgment when they ask for or seek advice. Led by such motivations, we end up isolating ourselves, thinking it's solely our duty to solve our problems and help others at the same time. We can become so obsessed with having all the answers, we can even begin to shut out those moments of doubt we have about ourselves. Essentially, we feel we have to be everything to everyone, and that leaves us alone, with no one there who actually knows us. This is not healthy. No one can function without help from others; none of us are invincible.

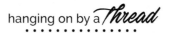

No one can function without help from others; none of us are invincible.

This is a problem I know all about. Some years ago, I faced a number of challenges all at once in my church and personal life. The city wanted to build up and revamp a new community center right where our church sat. They didn't seem to take our presence or our needs into account, and we had to consider the option of moving. During that planning time, I was also going through some personal struggles. My son was diagnosed with a serious illness and treatment options were limited. Meanwhile, I, too, faced a critical surgery. Despite being an adult with many years of experience under my belt, I felt backed into a corner regarding the decisions I needed to make; I felt forced into some of them. Ultimately, we actually had to move the church and build somewhere else and we had to build under a serious time constraint. It was a big decision, and a hard one to focus on at times due to the issues in my personal life. So much would change, and so much would need to move. I felt a real responsibility to my community and to my congregation; and of course, there were obvious responsibilities to my family as well. With all of this barely thought through, I moved forward. My church spent five years making the move happen, and my family faced the illnesses. It was hard, both on me and my wife and on others, especially on my son. I went from feeling settled and in control to handling challenges daily just to keep my family and congregation going. Because I was so overwhelmed, my wife had to absorb many new responsibilities, responsibilities I never wanted to place on her. I asked myself every day if I was making the right decisions, if I had done the right thing for my family and my church. Self-doubt became a regular, uninvited activity. Many of us in leadership positions fall into this habit of second-guessing. We have many decisions to make on a daily basis, but we question our own authority, and we undermine our own ability to make and feel good about our decisions. We make it worse by internalizing everything and allowing it to fester.

In that time of struggle, I felt that no one could possibly understand what I was going through. I felt alone facing those, and possibly other, future challenges. I felt lost and overwhelmed. After all, I had been hit with so many troubles in such a short period of time, there were sure to be more. This loneliness only increased because I could not always find the words to express the feelings. At the worst possible time, in that moment of desperation, I hid my struggles from the outer world. I do believe my wife could see the pressure building, but gave me the space and the peace to work my way through it, thinking that's what I needed. I could not find a way to ask her and others for more support. My personality allows me to keep a calm and gregarious façade. For others, their pain might be more visible. In many ways, my personality is the more dangerous one. Like myself, plenty of people can make it look like everything is fine when it isn't, and they are harder to reach and harder to help. They are also the ones we need to be most concerned about. In my case, I kept the smile on my face, but I did eventually begin to realize that I was truly **holding on by a thread**. My faith, my personality, and my ability to accomplish the tasks before me without faltering saved me from depression or isolation, but as I wrote my sermons and preached perseverance, I was preaching to myself. I became acutely aware that I was in need of some direction; I needed a way back. I took some time to reflect and some time to reach out to others to gauge how I was feeling and to find the techniques necessary to master my situation and find a path towards recovery. In this way, I was quite blessed. Not everybody can do this.

REACHING THE BREAKING POINT

Going through painful situations never feels "normal." While we are in the midst of the storm, it feels as if no one else has ever experienced pain in the same way. But feeling that way is, in fact, normal. It is normal for people to feel alone or isolated, to believe that no one really cares or ever will care. As I tell my story now, with over a decade of new challenges and experiences put behind me, I still feel the loneliness of my pain from all those years ago, but now I know that many other people can echo those same sentiments. In truth, we can frequently become isolated by the reality of the weight we have to bear, with our busy lives often requiring us to be silent about our personal challenges. Anyone who holds a position of responsibility over others knows this loneliness and struggle. Because we are leaders with reputations for resolve and fortitude, we bear it all alone, manufacturing those smiles and keeping those troubling emotions in check. Most of the time, when we have so much going on, we are ready to bubble over and explode, but we won't allow ourselves the luxury of expressing the overwhelming emotions we feel. We do not seek out those who may be able to help bring us through the storm of troubling feelings or the pressures on our public and personal lives.

We simply face it all alone.

Going through painful situations never feels "normal."

Then, even when we have already reached the breaking point, we are again called to help with something. These situations can bring about a fever pitch of emotions that we try to repress even further, thus putting ourselves in particularly dangerous positions. When someone feels like there is no end in sight to the pain and isolation, he or she may do something rash and terrible, simply because the stress and the constant barrage of challenges has left him or her bereft, a shell of who he or she used to be. What is worse, we are often incapable of seeing ourselves running down this treacherous path because artificial smiles and constant busyness are part of the coping mechanisms built into leaders and doers. We often say: "I'm OK. I'm fine. God is good. I don't need any help. How are YOU doing?"

This is particularly difficult in ministry and caring professions. There have been numerous clergy deaths due to suicide over the years. Hopefully, this warning will allow the rest of us to take note and ask ourselves important questions about the stress and strain that we put on ourselves. Unfortunately, I suspect that most of us will dismiss any thoughts of "I can't do this" or "I need to slow down" or even "I need to delegate more." Further, we will dismiss more serious thoughts like "I'm in trouble," "I'm suffering," or "I need help." Recent studies indicate that due to the ongoing economic crises and congregations' resistance to necessary change or cultural movements, pastors are feeling increased pressure from all sides and succumbing to depression. I'm sure this is true across the board in all areas of the professional and private world. It appears that over time, the economic issues that we all experience can take their toll and add up, even when they seem like "normal" or small day-to-day challenges. We all need to realize that the stresses of work and responsibility—ministry or not—are real and do affect us in many ways. And the stress is telling us that we need to adapt to the change that is front and center in our lives.

There are deeper issues within all of us, too, that can contribute to this pressure. Most of us feel that we are self-actualized people ready for any challenge—leaders who have no business asking for help. As leaders, however, we need to remember that in our positions of authority, we often watch out for these very issues in others. We advise others and directly discuss the issues involved in their work or private lives that prevent them from feeling joyful and force them to deal with bad feelings and move on. We need to do the same for ourselves.

AT THE ROOT OF OUR FRUSTRATION

It is hard for most of us to admit that we do care whether or not people, first, know us inside and out, and second, care about us. We like to think that we don't need anyone; we're tough, we can handle it all on our own. But really, we're just running away from confronting those two things. We need to bring all of our problems front and center and address them; this is how we can get through, how we can handle everything and emerge victorious from the trappings of stress or depression that take us to those dark places where we feel overwhelmed and lost.

We live somewhere between the expectations of others and ourselves and the reality of who we are able to be. In my own life, I feel that I stayed anxious longer than I should have during those difficult times years ago. Of course, I had reason to be, as I explained above. But at that same moment, I also had many reasons to feel blessed; I just did not see them as clearly. I was in a position to head a project at the church, so I did have professional success and the respect that goes with it. I had loved ones around me, and we were blessed to have some medical options along with the love and support of family and friends. But it is hard to see all that is good when so much feels bad. Many of you, I am sure, have been in that position. Professional success and personal happiness can become traps of their own. We can wake up and realize we are ensnared in a life we don't understand anymore, acting like a person we aren't sure we are anymore. We have good jobs, but those positions and respect bring additional responsibilities that shackle us to a life that doesn't quite fit like it used to. We have wives, husbands, and children, but we have to provide for them and care for them, sometimes sacrificing our own needs. We are torn between two responsibilities, the one we have to others and the one we have to ourselves. And in times of struggle, we can forget all the blessings behind those responsibilities, instead seeing impossible demands and a false sense of self where we should see love, respect, and comfort.

We live somewhere between the expectations of others and ourselves and the reality of who we are able to be.

In my case, I was beginning to feel that I was in a box that was designed and built for somebody else. I felt frustrated and lost. More than anything, I felt angry, and I didn't want to acknowledge that anger. Most of us are well-acquainted with this kind of anger, and like me, we just don't want to admit it's there. When we are **holding on by a thread**, this anger—along with anxiety and sadness—threatens to take over. I will freely admit that this happened to me. I was angry back then, thinking that at my age, I should have been enjoying the fruits of my labors, my family, my church and congregation, and all my successes born of years of hard work. Instead, I was battling on all fronts. At home, I was trying to make sure that we were a solid support system with encouragement and comfort while dealing with a sickness I did not understand and could not fix. At work, I was struggling with a large building project that would take years. Looking back, I was angry at the very church to which I had once felt so close. I was angry at the expectations of my church. I was angry that the church had to always take the high ground and point the way. I was angry at what I perceived as an "invisible church" imposing theology and doctrines onto all of us that didn't necessarily help us or free us in tough moments. This invisible church only adds stress because, in order to obey it, we often feel that we have to deny who we are or what we really need. I felt judged by the church that was supposed to help me. I was also extremely angry at the "visible church," the brick and mortar structure that sat where it wasn't supposed to sit, or the church that had to be built using time and money that tapped our resources as an organization. On top of all that, I was personally tapped out, and there was no time for rest and relaxation. I struggled to see a way out that would still allow me to offer the additional help my loved ones so desperately needed. It was maddening, and these feelings of anger only served to feed depression.

As a pastor, it was hard for me to even approach the subject that I might theoretically feel disillusioned with church doctrine. Because, where was I, if that was the case? More importantly, who was I? In my world, at that time, there was no room to bend, no chance to change. If it wasn't all, it was nothing, and I was afraid with just that little more put on my shoulders, I would break. But this, too, was a normal part of the process. I think we can all admit that sometimes life can make us feel like prisoners and victims of those things we are closest to, especially if we are in leadership roles. Preaching liberation to others when we feel that we are in bondage can make us feel victimized. Over time, this will build resentment and the feelings of helplessness or depression that I described earlier. Where we want to turn our restlessness into progress, we are instead forced to conform to rigid old standards. Where we want to think more about being true to ourselves, we instead must fight to remain ourselves within what we advocate from a position of leadership. We pastors know what it is to wrestle with a generation that wants to explore new ideas and approaches while we wait for an old institution to catch up to that kind of thinking. John the Baptist notoriously showed up at gatherings wearing camel-hair clothes and eating bugs and jelly, free to be himself with no one questioning his motives or actions. In the modern church, and in modern business and society, we do not have the privilege of shocking the system like that, and that can be frustrating. In essence, as leaders we are expected by everyone to be the composite view of the eternal Christ. This is true in family, business, and religion. It is a tall order and, often, one that does not make us comfortable. We are, after all, only human.

WHAT IS SCANDALOUS FOR LEADERS MAY BE NORMAL BEHAVIOR FOR EVERYONE ELSE

Church leaders, in particular, often have a hard time remembering that we are only human. We hold ourselves to such high standards because we think others expect the same of us. This is a fault of the profession, but it is not exclusive to the church. I know that the expectation of being more than human comes with a lot of careers.

However, regardless of our walks of life, we need to remember that while we are expected to have grown and settled into our positions as leaders, we often still have growth and development of our own to handle. While we are watching over the growth and the plans for happiness and success of others, we too are growing, learning, and evolving. This is normal. Yet, in our respective positions, we are told that it is not.

Part of this comes from the fear that a change in how we see ourselves will lead to uncomfortable growing pains. Indiscretions and mistakes of any kind are huge scandals for preachers, and only slightly lesser ones for others in positions of high authority, while for those with less responsibility, they are simply considered minor "blips" that are easily forgiven. For others, these indiscretions are something they will get through with only a cut or bruise. For us preachers, it is something that can ruin us. As Christians, we firmly believe that Jesus Christ came in the flesh to set us free, but as we focus on the process of expressing that freedom and becoming our own person just like everyone else, we find that we are held to a different standard. Further, sometimes to our own surprise, we find that we hold ourselves to even higher standards still. Jesus came in the flesh for a reason. He came, in part, to show us that we are not infallible, that we are instead prone to mistakes and need the explorations and forgiveness found in friendship, loyalty, faith, and so much more. Life is about growth, struggle, overcoming, coming through, and emerging closer to God through Christ as much as ever before. It is about meeting Him in all our challenges and changes and knowing that, as we often hear, "our trials only come to make us strong." Yet, few leaders feel as if they have the privilege to make the mistakes others make in their process of becoming. The boss has to help the employee get through some sticky places. The father has to help the child over a mountain of mistakes. Leaders, on the other hand, are often out there by themselves, shunned by those who get a peek into the laboratory of their development. In short, we offer freedom to others, yet feel ourselves bound and restricted. As the late theologian, pastor, and activist Dr. Prathia Hall once said, "It's hard to preach liberation and live in bondage."

This expected perfectionism is bad enough, but it is all the harder to live with because it makes most of us feel that people just simply do not know us at all. In this virtual world, people do not always take the time to really get to know others. I have heard so many people voice that they have an ache in their spirit because they feel alone. I have heard leaders talk about what they do for others, and yet, the same is seldom done for them. They are expected to know what their group or team needs and wants, but seldom does the team or group reciprocate. What is more frustrating is that people think they DO know us, at least in our positions as leaders. How can they, when our deeper feelings and needs are kept under wraps deliberately because, of all things, those feelings are too human for the people in our lives to handle? We are not meant to have human needs or to make human mistakes; we are meant to guide, forgive, manage, direct, and strengthen others. It is hard for others to view us as leaders and at the same time also know the full weight of our real struggles. Every parent has realized this truth when they have consciously chosen to keep something from their children. Our struggles are normal; we just need to be able to acknowledge them and handle them as we see fit, which is what we often offer to others. We are men and women of authority, and that is how we are perceived, viewed, interacted with, and understood. Many times, however, we feel more like the Wizard of Oz, a man who preacher, scholar, and speaker Dr. Frank Thomas reminds us is "the little man behind the curtain, pushing buttons, and pulling knobs." I know that when I feel that way or feel that I am **hanging on by a thread**, the weight of everything is compounded by the knowledge that I am in it by myself.

However, there's an answer to the feeling of being lost and alone. The truth is, no one can know you until you know you, the you in this very moment. That's the you of today, not the you of twenty years ago when you started down this road. In the chapters ahead, we will work through a system that allows us to embrace the world around us and the world within, to find ourselves and to reach out to others. Throughout our process, we will examine how to get to know ourselves, and we will use that knowledge to better our life experiences and those of others when we are in the position to guide them. After all, no matter what we do—heads of an industry, pastors of churches, community leaders, ministry leaders, heads of a family—we still need something to reach for whenever we are **hanging on by a thread**. And we will soon find that in the THREAD Principle.

*I know that when I feel that way or feel that I am **hanging on by a thread**, the weight of everything is compounded by the knowledge that I am in it by myself.*

BREAKOUT SESSION WITH BISHOP THOMAS:

Hanging On By a Thread: Living with Mistakes as a Leader

Think about a problem you experienced either in past years or recently. What was it about that problem, incident, or experience that shut you down or upset you to the point of questioning yourself and your existence or your role as a leader?

_____

_____

_____

_____

_____

_____

_____

_____

_____

_____

_____

_____

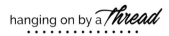

Define "crisis." What do you feel, think, or picture when you say or write that word down? Have you ever had a crisis? Do you feel that you have never had a crisis?

_____

_____

_____

_____

_____

_____

_____

_____

_____

_____

_____

_____

_____

_____

In this chapter, I mention four areas that I feel significantly impact our emotions, and more specifically what causes our ups and downs and eventually our ultimate happiness. What are these areas and how do you personally feel each one affects your life? Maybe one area applies to you but another does not.

_____

_____

_____

_____

_____

_____

_____

_____

_____

_____

_____

_____

_____

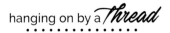
Have you made a big mistake or mistakes in your life? Do you have regrets or often think about situations or occurrences that bother you? First, I want you to detail those thoughts here, putting the emphasis on your feelings, and then I want you to spend equal time telling yourself (and writing it here) what you learned from your mistakes or experiences and how going through such things will help you and those you are responsible for in the future.

_____

_____

_____

_____

_____

_____

_____

_____

_____

_____

_____

_____

_____

Think back to the times when you made those big mistakes. Did you feel alone? Was there anyone you felt you could trust? Why didn't you reach out to people? Do you think the burden would have been lessened if you had reached out?

_____

_____

_____

_____

_____

_____

_____

_____

_____

_____

_____

_____

_____

_____

CHAPTER **TWO**

· · · · · · · · · · · · · · · · · · · ·

Self-Actualization: The Journey to Rediscovering You

What do we mean when we say we have lost ourselves? We are, after all, just where we always were. We still see ourselves in the mirror every morning. We still greet the same family at the breakfast table. We still go off to the same job and act in the same leadership roles. We still drive the same car and return to the same home. In every part of our lives we are very much found just where we are expected to be. How, then, can we be lost?

When we say we're lost, what we mean is we are not living the life we feel we are meant to be living. We wake up the same person that we were the night before but now something just doesn't seem to fit. Essentially, we have fallen off the ladder of self-actualization, and we can't seem to find our way back on.

Self-actualization, according to the late American psychologist Abraham Maslow, is a primary human need. Our desire for personal fulfillment is so central to our identity, Maslow describes it as our quest to fulfill our highest needs. This desire to have and discover meaning and purpose is the cherry on top of a satisfied life. It motivates us and guides us. In his work, Maslow compares the existential search for fulfillment, which is often represented as a pyramid, to a journey that we take through life in which we first attempt to fulfill our basic human needs and then allow our quest for actualization to prompt us to expand our horizons. He describes this search as innate, one that we are incomplete without. Essentially, for us to fully function, self-actualization needs to be a priority in our lives. And when we lose that, we lose ourselves. That's when we find we are **hanging on by a thread**.

As Christians, we would add that our greatest need is a belief in and a relationship with God. In fact, we know that unity with Him and the act of seeking a higher spirituality in our "oneness" with Him is actually the most crucial part of this self-actualizing priority. Yet, no matter how deeply we know this, if we are struggling elsewhere, it can be hard to concentrate on reaching out to God. In such moments, we are constantly pulled back by our more basic needs and the emotional impact they have on us. We tumble down the pyramid and take steps backward on our journey as we struggle with worries about health and safety, our self-esteem, and our physiological and spiritual needs. These inner needs rise up against us and haunt us when they go unfulfilled, pulling us away from our highest aims of spiritual development and self-actualization.

> *As Christians, we would add that our greatest need is a belief in and a relationship with God.*

But how did we get here? Yesterday, when we woke up, we were happy with ourselves and our path in life. Today, it all feels wrong. The truth is that our actualization is constantly in flux. Success and meeting our needs doesn't happen in a straight line. It is not a single, static event, declared and then done. We don't buy milk once and consider the deed done forever. Next week, we need another carton. Likewise, we don't choose a single identity and live with it for our whole lives. We constantly have to return to our pyramid and address each block. Self-actualization requires a difficult journey, an emotional and mental journey, one that at times feels overwhelming. As I mentioned in the last chapter, for us—leaders—it is all the more difficult. We are called to help others when we cannot help ourselves. And in the midst of helping others to shape and form their lives, we feel as if we are losing control of our own.

Maslow defines self-actualization as "the desire for self-fulfillment, namely to the tendency for [the individual] to become actualized in what he is potentially" (*Maslow, 1954, Motivation and Personality,* p. 93). Or, more pithily, "What a man can be, he must be." Yet, we are constantly trying to be what we can be in the midst of circumstances and situations that act against us. In other words, while we seek to discover our full potential, other circumstances are seeking to pull us off track. While we are trying to discover our potential, the very ground under our feet is shifting. And that's before we even consider our role as Christians and leaders, where an even higher directive is laid on us. God told the prophet Ezekiel, *"Son of man, I have made you a watchman for the people of Israel"* (Ezekiel 33:7), to warn the people of impending danger. In doing so, He laid out the directive that we do not have the luxury to just live life and muddle through its rough spots with concern only for ourselves. As Christians, we have to find meaning and then share that meaning with those who look to us for answers.

Maslow's Hierarchy
OF NEEDS

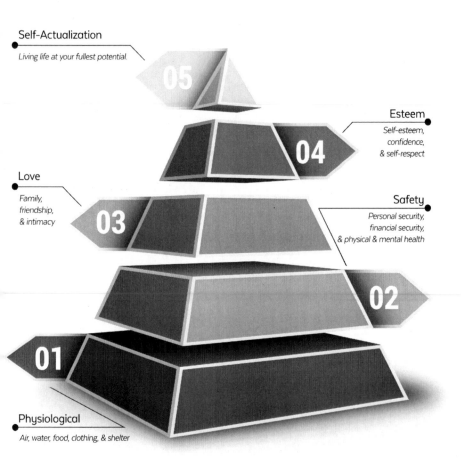

Self-Actualization

Living life at your fullest potential.

05

Esteem

*Self-esteem,
confidence,
& self-respect*

04

Love

*Family,
friendship,
& intimacy*

03

Safety

*Personal security,
financial security,
& physical & mental health*

02

01

Physiological

Air, water, food, clothing, & shelter

While we are trying to discover our potential, the very ground under our feet is shifting.

The conflict between our needs and the needs of those we are responsible for is something I know more than a little about, as I have mentioned. A number of years ago, I was put in a nearly impossible situation with difficulties at church and in my body. When I first got the test results that told me I would need surgery, I was stopped in my tracks. I already felt overworked because the church had hit a growth spurt and we were firing on all cylinders. At the time, I was 39 and married with three children, one an infant. I must admit, I was overwhelmed by the fear that the situation might end tragically. Still, I had to preach, teach, and minister while visiting the doctor for more tests. I was what Henri Nouwen called "a wounded healer." I was trying to follow my journey to self-actualization, to press for the top, to work toward a closer relationship with God, but all the while I was struggling with the very issues at the base of the hierarchy of needs pyramid: my own survival.

Sometimes, life and the pursuit of self-actualization can become overwhelming. In such moments, we are challenged on all fronts. It's not like we can't handle a little challenge now and then; it's just that, during particularly difficult times, we can't get any rest because we attempt to handle too much all at once—our responsibilities to our career and community, our family, and also ourselves. The Prophet Elijah wrestled with this as he fled from the presence of Ahab and Jezebel. After reaching the desert of Beersheba, he lay down and slept under a broom tree. His spirit and mind were beginning to show the wear and tear of his mission. In the morning, when he awoke, there was food for him to eat and an angel of the Lord standing by to tell him, *"Get up and eat, for the journey is too much for you"* (1 Kings 19:7). In such desperate moments, when we are **hanging on by a thread**, God has to remind us that the journey is, indeed, too great for us, that we need a little assistance to get back on the right path. That cuts at the core of our capabilities and our competencies as leaders and doers, but it also reminds us of the enormity of the work God has assigned us and that God does not mean for us to bear it alone.

The journey to self-actualization, the quest for inner meaning and purpose, is a quest that guides and governs our lives. As Christians, we want to be all that God intends for us to be. It is the vision that awakens us in the morning and that guides us throughout the day. It fires our creative juices and it fuels our faith. But even within our community of faith, others do not always understand this compelling drive. Some say, "Christians are here to serve and serving takes precedent (over growing)." A fine and obvious truth on paper, but we all struggle with trying to actualize our potential as servants to become all God intended in the face of other obligations. At such moments, the requirement to serve others runs headlong into the personal desire to grow. Who will we be? Martha who waits tables so all are taken care of, or Mary who sits at the Master's feet for her own development and growth?

As Christians, we want to be all that God intends for us to be.

Our need to serve others is probably the reason many of us seldom allow ourselves to take even a few days off. How often does a day off mean just taking our work home or getting some off-the-clock research taken care of? How often does it mean taking care of family responsibilities and housekeeping that we too often neglect? How many of us smuggle in an informal business lunch or try to tie our outings in with our larger commitments to our church, our business, or our committee? If we ever do take time off, we make sure to pay it back somewhere, making it up with late evenings or weekend hours, so that all that rest is paid back with additional work. When this becomes too much, when health becomes involved—as in my case— or the obligations simply pile up beyond our abilities, how many of us ever actually reach out to friends or family or other professionals who work with people in matters of self-care to even discuss our problems, let alone mention that they are getting to be too much for us? I suspect that most of us go home at night and eat dinner while making pleasant conversation and then either keep ourselves up with our minds racing or bury our feelings of frustration by focusing on our children's, friend's, or spouse's concerns rather than our own. "How was YOUR day?" "How was school?" "How can I help YOU?" "What more can I do for YOU?"

Others may want us and even need us to be involved in their moment, but there are times it is the exact opposite of what we need. Nevertheless, to be good Christians, we always put ourselves in the position of confidante and advisor to those around us. We try to make ourselves available all the time. When our personal issues interfere, we set them aside with the expectation that we and we alone will solve them, which inevitably causes us great distress. The truth is, often we cannot just solve them. They require time and attention. Not that we are willing to acknowledge that. After all, our current habits have probably been in place for years. Resentments from childhood, traumas from adolescence, or unresolved issues from college have set in motion our approach to handling the thorny issues that rise in our lives. We have left so much unexamined, unexpressed, and unresolved. So much that was left unresolved in our growth is still very much present. Areas of hurt or need that were not fully addressed when we were younger are sure to rise up and haunt us once we occupy positions as parents, employers, and spiritual leaders that require a mastery of those old emotional burdens. How can anyone handle such a buildup of emotion, physical exhaustion, and constant input from others? Yet somehow, we all try to do it.

So, how do we find our way back? How do we get back to the point where the person we see in the mirror is the person we know again? How do we move past the point where no one truly knows us and we don't know ourselves and get back to the person we knew who became this leader in the first place?

To avoid these feelings of emptiness, we need to start by removing the "every" from our obligations. We don't need to be "everything to everybody," but "something to some people." It is only when we are able to face not just our goals but our limitations that we can be satisfied with what we are able to do in a day, a week, or a year. Then, we will no longer ask "what more can I do?" because we know, in our hearts and minds, that we have done what we are supposed to do. In this regard, we are not facing our needs and insecurities from a position of weakness. We are not feeling sorry for ourselves or feeling inadequate. We are recognizing and realizing that no matter how good a preacher, a businessperson, a parent, or a student we are, we too have needs and limitations that must be addressed. We too are mortal and it was God who made us mortal. We have to learn that we cannot give up everything about who we are and still recognize ourselves in the mirror in the morning. We cannot address everyone's every need, not only for our own sanity, but for those we are closest to. We force ourselves to live at a pace we cannot maintain, and we rob others of the authenticity from us that they do dearly desire.

This is not an idle point. It is hard to fulfill ourselves and to address the needs of others at the same time. Period. In fact, there have been moments in my life when I realized I had to slow down, or drop out of warp speed as I will refer to it later in this book, if the people around me were to survive. Our partners and families are not always built to travel as fast as we are traveling. If we do not have the strength of our own convictions to slow down and help them with their pain, we are failing them even if we think we aren't failing ourselves. I remember at one point in my career being so absorbed in work that I was traveling almost every week, all while my children were facing their own school-age crises and needed their daddy. They did not need the Superman of the church who could spin time backwards or perform superhuman feats; they needed *their daddy*. I had to drop out of warp speed and travel at their pace. That was a lesson I'll never forget.

That lesson doesn't just apply to our families. We have a tendency to warp past the people we work with too. They try to keep up, unaware of what is driving us and forcing us from some level of normalcy into the abnormal. In fact, those around us often don't even know what normal should look like for us or for themselves. Most of us have been keeping an abnormal pace so long that everyone around us has defined it as our normal. We are drawing them into our craziness, our dysfunctionality, and our confusion.

It is only when we, like Elijah, acknowledge our limitations and slow down that God can work His miracles in our lives. It is only when we let God recalibrate our pain and our needs by telling us the journey is too great for us that we are able to return to a real normal. Prayerfully, it is not too late for us to take note of the problems we are causing others and ourselves. Our families and co-workers are trying to keep up in a race that we need to cancel. And by sitting one or two laps around the track out, we can begin to search for what has prompted such behavior in the first place. That doesn't mean we can't still push ourselves and reach for the skies, but it refocuses us on operating with God's glory in mind as well as our own journey to self-actualization.

A few years ago, my city was blanketed with snow. The city was shut down completely for days. Workplaces were closed, schools were closed, even markets and superstores were closed. In many areas, power outages left people without any electricity. Televisions sat black and cell phones could not be recharged. As a church, we had to work out forms of communication to make sure everyone was okay. Our team started out by making calls on old-school landlines to seniors. Then, once the power returned, we sent out video messages to families and individuals of all ages throughout the community. We did this because many people were becoming depressed. It was not SAD (seasonal affective disorder); these people were *becoming depressed* because they were being forced to slow down and think and feel their thoughts. Their jobs and hurried lives offered them a way to escape from dealing with the real issues that haunted them. They, too, had to finally look in the mirror and see how lost they felt. With all of those hiding places taken offline, their thoughts and feelings stepped forward, demanding time and attention. Yet, many emerged from the blizzard more whole and more ready to live because they had faced those thoughts and *"come forth as gold"* (Job 23:10).

By being forced to sit, struggle, and contemplate their needs, ambitions, and overall place in the world, some of the people in my community came through with a stronger sense of themselves. Clearly, knowing our own needs helps. Tapping into what we need and coming to grips with the fact that all of our issues are not immediately resolvable is of paramount importance. The advice we gain from others will be far more beneficial when this has become a reality we cease to ignore. I cannot stress this enough. By recognizing our limitations, we can slow down to face our own needs, limitations, and expectations more. Warp speed is our attempt to be or become everything to everyone *in spite of all of our own baggage.* That's a system we can't afford to keep living in, and changing it is imperative.

The truth is, we have to come to accept a very basic point about our human nature: we have to change or die. I don't mean this in the melodramatic sense that we will all expire if we don't change, but I do want us to seriously consider the consequences of the unresolved motivations that drive us to lose ourselves in others because we can't face ourselves. When we deny ourselves a sense of accomplishment, and a sense of our limitations, we are denying ourselves the chance to find our self. We risk losing sight of a well-balanced life and living with the frustration and anger that I brought up in the last chapter. This is an obvious component of the self-actualization journey, but it is a hard one to master. Living as others perceive us, how our church or business or family wants us to be, or how we idealize ourselves can be destructive but very addicting. Self-actualization, according to Maslow, is about what we "can be," what we are able to achieve. We have to be realistic here and give ourselves the right to change, to evolve to the person we are today from the person we were twenty years ago.

Believe me, I understand that none of this is easy. It's not easy to slow down, open ourselves up, and make real changes. We're used to living lives of sacrifice, of stretching ourselves thin to be everything to everybody. We're used to **hanging on by a thread**. We've all had to give up a great deal in life to get to where we are now. We've all made our mistakes and paid for them alone, all made our sacrifices and lived with them without complaint. Most of us are still making sacrifices. We feel forced in our roles as leaders to deny ourselves the opportunity to investigate the person we are today. We cower from the consequences of choices we might have to make and from the person we will have to introduce to the world. On some level, it seems so much easier to continue pretending, to continue moving at light-speed and being everything to everybody—the perfect, upstanding leader instead of the real, human man or woman. We fear what people will think. We fear that even the smallest mistake will shock the public. Yet, our fear will not bring us any closer to a sense of fulfillment. Our anger and frustration will not empower us to be comfortable with the false face we have created for the world. We must navigate the waters with a better plan. And to do that, we need worthy sailors at our side.

To that end, I have established a system to help all of us launch out and set a new course to meet the person we are today. In order to stop **hanging on by a thread**, we are going to have to **strengthen that thread** so we can get back on course for the journey to our self-actualization. And that's just what we're going to do, starting in the next chapter.

BREAKOUT SESSION WITH BISHOP THOMAS:

Hanging On By a Thread: Who Are You?

Detail some of your best qualities and some of your worst. Be honest and be analytical.

_____

_____

_____

_____

_____

_____

_____

_____

_____

_____

_____

_____

_____

Detail some of your hobbies and interests. Share some of your regrets. Try to see how the two lists are similar and how they are different. What are your observations?

_____

_____

_____

_____

_____

_____

_____

_____

_____

_____

_____

_____

_____

_____

Look again at that list of hobbies. How many of your close relationships are built off of these sorts of situations? How many are founded on genuine affection for one another?

_____

_____

_____

_____

_____

_____

_____

_____

_____

_____

_____

_____

_____

_____

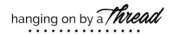

In this chapter, I mention Abraham Maslow and his hierarchy of needs. Does his theory speak to you and your current situation?

_____

_____

_____

_____

_____

_____

_____

_____

_____

_____

_____

_____

_____

_____

What are ten things that you want the people close to you to know about you that you have been afraid to share?

_____

_____

_____

_____

_____

_____

_____

_____

_____

_____

_____

_____

_____

_____

_____

CHAPTER **THREE**

· ·

Strengthening the Thread

So, we are ready to rediscover ourselves, to find our way back after some time in the wilderness. But how do we get ourselves into this process? We know we want to turn the pages of a bad chapter, but when we actually look at the practical side of moving forward, it suddenly doesn't seem so easy. Many times, we are so enmeshed in our daily lives that we are unable to break free of bad habits and destructive behaviors to honestly acknowledge our need to recalibrate our journey to self-actualization. These habits, after all, have become comfortable; they feel safe. Even when we open ourselves to exploring alternatives to these behaviors, we find ourselves falling back into that comfortable old routine that we've established.

Trying to set up a new, positive, and honest identity is difficult. We fear what others will think, we fear getting to know ourselves and letting others truly know us—know that we have been **hanging on by a thread**. That is why I have developed the THREAD Principle. The Principle outlines the practical steps that can be taken to restore balance to people's lives—people with good intentions living lives that have spun out of control. These steps help those leaders who have focused too much energy on others and allowed outside factors to influence their lives in ways that are no longer beneficial to growth.

The simple steps outlined in the THREAD Principle can lead to a more manageable and fulfilled life.

1. Take a Breath

2. Harmonize Your Different Selves

3. Reinvest in God

4. Extend Yourself

5. Accept Advice and Help

6. Discover and Develop You

In the following chapters, we will investigate each of these steps in detail as we slowly take our journey back to one of fulfilling self-actualization and away from the loneliness where no one knows us and we don't know ourselves. Each step is based on a solid foundation of psychological research and faith in God, reaching us through the mind and the spirit.

For now, though, what follows is a brief overview of each step.

THE THREAD PRINCIPLE STEP 1: TAKE A BREATH

I mentioned in chapter two the need for us to drop out of warp speed. This is an idea I learned from Pete Scazzero, founder of New Life Fellowship Church, a large, multiracial, international church in Queens, New York. When we are going faster than 186,000 miles per second all the time, we are going to fail, collapse, or work ourselves and those around us into a frenzy. As leaders, this goes double, as we try to be "everything to everybody." When we live at warp speed, we become so absorbed in what we are doing that we are unable to face the insecurity or sense of inadequacy that is driving us. We have to

THREAD

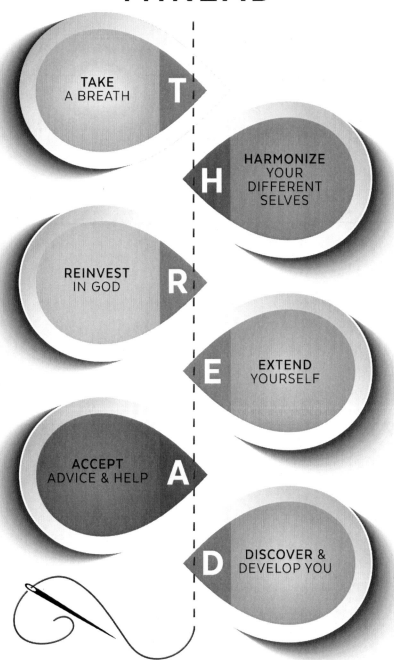

TAKE A BREATH

T

HARMONIZE YOUR DIFFERENT SELVES

H

REINVEST IN GOD

R

EXTEND YOURSELF

E

ACCEPT ADVICE & HELP

A

DISCOVER & DEVELOP YOU

D

learn to slow down and take a breath, or else risk **snapping that final thread** and plunging into emotional turmoil.

When we are going faster than 186,000 miles per second all the time, we are going to fail, collapse, or work ourselves and those around us into a frenzy.

THE THREAD PRINCIPLE STEP 2: HARMONIZE YOUR DIFFERENT SELVES

We may not always realize it, but we do not have a single "identity" but a combination of many different "selves" all thrown together. Every hat we wear defines the person that we are at that time, and we can wear many hats on any given day. When we don't pay attention to these different pieces of our identity, we can find ourselves losing our sense of self and end up struggling to act like a cohesive whole. In order to find our way back to that whole, we have to attend to each piece and put it back in its place first.

THE THREAD PRINCIPLE STEP 3: REINVEST IN GOD

Though this comes third in the principle, to any Christian, it is the most important step. We have to make sure who we are is aligned with who God wants us to be. We might consider this step the central anchor of the entire principle; all other parts flow through and to this point. For, as Paul said, *"in Him we live and move and have our being"* (Acts 17:28).

THE THREAD PRINCIPLE STEP 4: EXTEND YOURSELF

As we go through the steps of the THREAD Principle, we are constantly extending ourselves. We have to extend ourselves just to show the world we are slowing down to take a breath, and we are extending ourselves as we get to know our different selves. We are especially extending ourselves when we accept advice and help. But in this step, I have something very specific in mind: the need to extend ourselves out of our comfort zone and reach a little into our fear zone. With God on our side, we now have the courage to step away a bit from routine and find the person we are meant to be today, even if it is a bit scary.

THE THREAD PRINCIPLE STEP 5: ACCEPT ADVICE AND HELP

I learned long ago that advice is a lot like quinine: a marvelous cure for ailments but one that is bitter and hard to swallow. Of course, the treatment is better than the alternative, and the same holds true for advice. As leaders, we are often afraid to go to others for advice and help. We are so used to handing out the advice and being the helping hand, we are afraid what others will think. Advice is outside our comfort zones, and opening ourselves up to it can take some adjustment.

But once we do finally start to let others in to our personal struggles and allow them to help steer us forward and help take some of the burden, we find that we suddenly have the energy and drive to overcome what has kept us struggling internally for so long.

THE THREAD PRINCIPLE STEP 6: DISCOVER AND DEVELOP YOU

The final step is a matter of letting all that came before culminate in recognizing the you you are today. We have to recognize that life

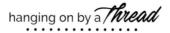
requires change and renewal, and by simply participating in that process, we are not acting against ourselves or betraying those we feel responsibility for. We have to let the THREAD steps guide us towards the person in the mirror. That person is not a stranger; that person is us. We have just lost track of ourselves.

We have to let the THREAD steps guide us towards the person in the mirror.

It is natural in life for everyone to have questions about their identity from time to time. We all want to be a success in life, but what defines success for us? What makes us feel like we are living successful, fulfilling lives? Is it the same definition as the one we had ten, fifteen, twenty years ago? Is it still all about money? A big house? Prestige? A high-level job? Or is it about family? Faith? Community? A chance to do something good and helpful for others? I think, if we consider it for a moment, we will find that our definition of success—and our self-image of ourselves as successful and fulfilled—has changed as we moved through life. We need to break the cycle of seeing ourselves through our outdated definitions. We have to stop **fraying away at the old thread** that held us together and start reinforcing it with the introspection and honesty found in the THREAD Principle.

There's nothing wrong with redefining ourselves as we are today, as seeing success as pure companionship and fellowship at work, church, and in neighborhoods and families. There's nothing wrong with defining our success as taking the time to truly appreciate the sunset and truly enjoy the sunrise. There's nothing wrong with a definition of success that includes working with the less fortunate and encouraging the left out. There's nothing wrong with success based on focusing on the needs of others who are hurting rather than our own wants of status symbols. The truth is that there is nothing wrong with any of these kinds of success. And all of them may be healthier for you and more appropriate for you than the definition you currently have. We have to stop measuring ourselves by our old yardsticks. The person you are today, faults and successes and all, doesn't have to fit the person you saw yourself as in the past.

There's nothing wrong with defining our success as taking the time to truly appreciate the sunset and truly enjoy the sunrise.

I maintain that, if we follow the THREAD Principle, we will finally learn to lead not just others but ourselves to a place where we are allowed to let our true selves shine forth, a place where new paths may present themselves that will bring satisfaction and fulfillment back into our lives. At the end of these new paths will be a greater and truer sense of success in life, however we define it. At the end will be self-actualization and a movement away from petty comparisons and stresses in our daily lives. We won't be as concerned about what people think of our hobbies, opinions, or lifestyles, or of our faults, because we will inherently know that we have made healthy and life-fulfilling choices that work.

The idea of discovery is gripping because it means something new is emerging into our consciousness. In a very real sense, something new is coming into being as we find ourselves through the THREAD Principle. A new chapter is beginning, and it is beginning for a newly

changed, different person. The gift that faith offers to us is the gift to be changed. Transformed. The disciples caught a glimpse of it on the Mount of Transfiguration when Jesus spoke with Moses and Elijah. They saw something "other." They discovered a Jesus that they had never seen before. The life that we are seeking is a life that gives us a self-image that is different from anything we have known. It is that journey that allows us to reach above **the break in the thread** and climb out of who we were and up into who we are called to become.

The idea of discovery is gripping because it means something new is emerging into our consciousness.

No one said this would be easy, but we must not stumble, we must not allow ourselves to take a step back. We need to take the time to understand ourselves so that we can show ourselves to the world with confidence, transforming into what we are meant to be. And we can do that by following the THREAD Principle. By taking this one step at a time, we can transform our lives to fit the people we are today. Now, *that* is true success.

BREAKOUT SESSION WITH BISHOP THOMAS:

Hanging On By a Thread: Strengthening that Thread!

What have you learned here? How can you implement the THREAD Principle into your life? Reiterate each step here and apply it to your own recalibration.

_____

_____

_____

_____

_____

_____

_____

_____

_____

_____

_____

_____

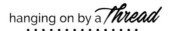
Where do you see yourself at the end of this year? In five years? In ten years? Talk about these goals in detail here. How is this future self different from the self you present now? Think about your career, family life, personal life, and spiritual life.

_____

_____

_____

_____

_____

_____

_____

_____

_____

_____

_____

_____

_____

What are the fears that have kept you from changing? If you were completely free from the fear of judgment from others, what would you change about yourself today?

_____

_____

_____

_____

_____

_____

_____

_____

_____

_____

_____

_____

_____

How do you think others see you? How do you think they would see a changed you if you implemented the changes above? Take it a step further by talking a bit about how you can make this hypothetical transition easier on yourself and others in your professional and personal life.

_____

_____

_____

_____

_____

_____

_____

_____

_____

_____

_____

_____

_____

CHAPTER **FOUR**

· · · · · · · · · · · · · · · · · · · ·

Take a Breath: Dropping Out of Warp Speed

As we begin our journey through the THREAD Principle, we have to take care of the very obvious but surprisingly challenging step for us leaders: we have to slow down and take a breath.

It all starts with how little time we give ourselves and how hard we press ourselves. I have already mentioned Peter Scazzero's thoughts on warp speed. Not only did he introduce the idea of warp speed to the discussion of modern living, he incisively said, "When you live your life at warp speed, expect to have a warped life." In other words, when we push the engines of our lives to their limits, we should expect to see breakdowns in the system. In our respective positions, we have put our systems under tremendous stress on many levels. The prevailing culture has taught us that the key to having everything is not only to be at the top of our game, but to be at the TOP of the top of our game, above and beyond anyone else, and even beyond our own expectations and abilities. To achieve this, we have cranked our accelerators up so high that we are blasting past life, all the while ignoring the fires in the engine room.

Our detrimental behavior has consequences beyond us; we aren't just warping our lives, of course. To make life run the way we feel we are meant to, we often stress out our co-workers, our families, our friends, and anyone who comes into contact with us. The whole of our world becomes stressed, and this is the very thing that we try to avoid by taking on so much ourselves. After all, being at the top of our game should mean that we should enjoy the fruits of our labor. But we don't. We can't. We are often so revved up that we don't know what to do when we do have the opportunity to slow down. We just push and push harder on that accelerator. We push to excel for the sake of excelling without even trying to tap into our true strengths or acknowledge basic human weaknesses; we push to hold ourselves to standards that are impossible to achieve, let alone maintain.

We hope all this pushing will allow us to perform at our very best, yet when we are moving at warp speed and stressed to the point of breaking, we actually make it more difficult for ourselves to sustain any sort of success or sense of improvement. That's not to say all this stress is bad. Sometimes, nervous anticipation or an adrenaline rush can be a sign of "eustress," or "positive stress." As we prepare to give a presentation or an important speech, nervous energy can directly contribute to a good end result. Many times, musicians or athletes come alive during concerts or athletic contests because a rush of adrenaline helps push them to work harder and achieve an optimal outcome. Obviously, this is not everyday stress; this stress is an exception, not the rule. Leaders under constant pressure are not just living on bursts of eustress. We push ourselves so hard so often, we reach the point of distress, and our performance suffers directly because of it.

So, what are we supposed to do? The answer is in the title (and in the first letter of THREAD): *take a breath*. Slow down, stop what you're doing, and take a breath. Breathe. For the first time in all those warped years, breathe in and out and let your responsibilities take a break for a minute. The reality is that, no matter how strong and motivated we are, we need to recharge, we need to re-evaluate what is good for us, and we need to rest. We have to breathe! The need to take a step back is particularly necessary for those of us in visible or public positions. The tension associated with always being in the spotlight adds another level of stress, and the consequences of having a breakdown in public are severe. For those who live this way, it is imperative that we get some sort of reprieve or rest.

The reality is that, no matter how strong and motivated we are, we need to recharge, we need to re-evaluate what is good for us, and we need to rest.

Does this apply to you? Almost certainly. I can prove it by asking you one simple question: "When is the last time you took a day off?" Dr. Joe Ratliff, Senior Pastor of the Brentwood Baptist Church in Houston, Texas has suggested, "We ought to take a day off every week, a week off every month, and a month off every year." Most of us would say that given the breakneck speed of our days, weeks, and years, taking time off would be ideal, but unfortunately, not realistic. In fact, at the very suggestion of taking a day or a week off, we often pick up the pace just to prove we can. We take on an extra shift or load ourselves down with extra work that could have otherwise stayed at the office. Through our own doing, we end up driving ourselves harder and faster than ever before. That behavior is just not sustainable. When Peter Scazzero says that we will live warped lives at this pace, his claim doesn't indicate that it is wrong to want more and to put in the hard work to achieve it; he is just reminding us that with all our stress, something is going to give, and it's going to give in a big way. Many times, if we don't stop to take a breath and reevaluate our lives, what has to give is the thing we most want to protect and keep whole: our families.

Refusing to take a breath has its consequences. In his book *Generation to Generation: Family Process in Church and Synagogue,* the late Rabbi Edwin Friedman makes the point that we often miss the real problems afflicting our families because we center on who has the problem, instead of focusing on where the stress is coming from. Where does it come from? Why does it exist? How do we fix it? We might focus on helping our spouses deal with both their stress and ours, or making sure our kids are thriving despite the hectic nature of our own lives. We might very well focus as much of our time and attention as we can on a problem when it presents itself, but we don't even touch—let alone resolve—the underlying factors at the core of the problems in the first place: *our living at warp speed.*

That doesn't mean we're not interested in dealing with these issues should we come upon them; they just aren't always readily apparent when we're blazing through life. Many families with a member in a high position have perfected the art of being a family on stage, and that involves getting very good at hiding family troubles. In other words, they show a united front to those who will judge them and gauge their success on how well they handle everything from their family lives to their personal finances. This is not an ideal life for any family unit, no matter how supportive, and stress is compounded by our failure to give our families the attention they need. That attention is instead given to the public, to our businesses, organizations, or our church, and to anyone else who is part of the success of that public persona. Many times, these relationships formed outside the family are not nearly as healthy and stable as we think them to be. They tend to add even more stress to our lives and more hours drawn away from those we care most about. In turn, the family suffers, and family members end up attending dinners, vacations, and other events on their own. In many cases, people end up lonely, lost, and feeling like they are moving so fast that they are unable to slow down and ask for directions back to the life they want to be living. People end up missing out on crucial opportunities to connect with their families and closest friends. They also miss the increased pressure building within their own support systems.

We all took measures to prepare ourselves for these types of challenges. We took classes or we became apprentices as we moved up the ranks. However, all the classes, experience, and time spent with mentors could not show us the truth: we were still at best observers to the lifestyle, still outsiders. We were part of the clamoring masses of people and organizations over whom our mentors had to spread their time. Preparing for the rigors of a life of leadership and its impact on our mental health—as well as the health of those closely connected to us—was not something that concerned us because the rigors and impact seemed much more manageable from the outside. As a result, we ended up unprepared for mounting challenges, for the gradual loss of time to even breathe, particularly as we gained more success and therefore picked up even more speed in our daily lives. Now, we don't really know how to stop the momentum. Further, for most of us, when we look around for an additional level of support, we find it is lacking. We expected something different from family life, something similar to what we saw growing up. In our minds, we had an idealized vision of a family full of comfort, where time slowed down and stress melted away. We did not know then as we do now: those families are simply more adept than our own at hiding their particular dysfunctions.

This can be a particularly lonely revelation to take in, especially since when we ask others who are in similar positions how "things" are going, we always get a positive response. When we specifically ask how their families are, they feel obligated to say that everything is fine. Sometimes, they are so busy moving at that warp speed that they really do think everything is fine when it is not. Other times, they are just wearing that public face we also wear, the one with the calm and encouraging smile, the one that offers service and help instead of asking for it. With the level of perfection we all expect from ourselves and the image of perfection we see around us, we have a hard time admitting when "things" are not great.

As I pointed out before, it is dangerous to ignore this pain and stress. Whether we want to admit it or not, we all know that stress is building and will eventually show up somewhere. I remember well how this manifested itself when my children were little. My daughter, Joi, would ask when I was coming home. My son, Walter, Jr., would ask why I wasn't home like other daddies. My other son, Joshua, would ask me about my availability on certain dates, never saying that he desperately wanted me to attend an event and support him. If I happened to be in town, Joshua might tell me about an important event that week. If I was away, I would hear from my other two children, both asking where I was and why my work was so important and time-consuming. They were asking me to take a breath and slow down and reprioritize and be with them. It bothered me at the time, but I knew I had aspirations and obligations to the ministry. Looking back at it now, I clearly had it wrong. Goals aside, I had to support a family too and I was leaving my wife with responsibilities that should have been shared. I thought my family would just understand and fall in line. Yet, that is a tall order for children below the age of fifteen and a wife who thought she would have greater support. And I made things worse by taking most of whatever free hours I had and dedicating them to the work of the church; I would sacrifice time designated for my family. After all, they were doing well on the surface, and so was I.

There's a reason the THREAD Principle starts out with taking a breath. Our inability to slow down and look at the world around us is a large part of why we find ourselves off the path of self-actualization today. It is also the only way to start the process of discovering who we are today. We have to take the time to stop what we're doing, breathe, and look at our life for what it is. Refusing to do this can lead to serious consequences. You are probably already living some of them, but continuing to warp through life will only lead to more devastating results as that last thread frays.

There's a reason the THREAD Principle starts out with taking a breath.

Honestly, the psychological dissonance that our schedules can produce can cause even the best of us to pursue behaviors that are not in anyone's best interests. We can become distant, defiant, dismissive, and even disappointing. To some extent, sometimes that is the best we can hope for. Keep in mind that the flesh always wins when the mind does not have an answer. So, to avoid the draw of our worst nature, we need to step back a little. We need to breathe and **strengthen the thread**. It was only when I dropped out of warp speed and took a breath that I learned to face my issues head on, see what problems I had created, and adjust the situation as soon as possible. After that revelation, I remember catching planes in the middle of ministry obligations to get home for a program or calling my wife three or four times a day and talking at length. It was an effort to show my family that they really were important to me, and it was an effort that I am grateful I put forth. Even with the best intentions, if we don't take time to slow down and show our families we appreciate them, we create ugly and monstrous situations. And as the situation deteriorates, we become increasingly afraid to see the problem at all. An old cliché says it best: "We have created the monster but don't want to call it ugly." How could we have made such mistakes? How could we ignore the pain of so many or allow so many negative occurrences? Warp speed, that's how.

Eventually, after I realized my token efforts weren't enough, I did call that monster ugly. I remember finally making the decision to scale back my preaching. Finally, I made sure that I was home every night doing things with my family and addressing all the issues that I had been putting off, the issues that were important to making us successful and happy as a unit. I went to work on redefining a structure that had gotten warped out of shape. Finally, I could see that clearly. The problem had been looking me in the face for a long time. I was traveling at warp speed and no one else could keep up. I had to drop out of warp speed and fly with the family at impulse speed. I needed to slow down, breathe, and create nurturing relationships that allowed my family and those close to me to see what love really looked like. I truly had to establish myself in the moment. I worked to be fully present every day. I gave every bit of attention to truly *being there* in mind, spirit, emotion, and body. And I enjoyed it. I found a place where I wasn't expected to travel at warp speed, and I was with the people I loved who really did not want to travel at warp speed either.

I gave every bit of attention to truly being there in mind, spirit, emotion, and body. And I enjoyed it.

This is how healing and self-actualization start, but it is by no means the end of the process. Slowing down for others and for ourselves opens the door for rediscovering relationships and ourselves, but there's a long way to go yet. Still, it all has to start with taking that first breath. A warp speed life catches everyone up in its chaos and velocity, particularly those of us enmeshed in a life that is lived partially in the public eye. Most of us will experience at least a taste of what it's like to miss out on important events in life, and what it's like to completely forget what we ourselves need or want out of life and relationships. This type of lifestyle affects everyone around us, from our immediate family to our church, from our circle of friends to our staff members, to others close to us emotionally and personally, and it eventually affects our sense of self. Warp speed creates *a lot of debris*—what a friend of mine once referred to as the "burning wreckage" of a life lived too fast. Staying on course gets tougher and tougher as the speed increases and as the debris gets thick around us, until we notice it getting lodged in the engines and the whole craft starts going down.

A colleague once told me that after his father's death, he had to assume the pastoral reins. During this critical time, he was concentrating on bringing stability back to his ministry and the lives of others as a church leader, but he was never able to grieve for his father. He was moving so fast and trying to do so much all at once, that he didn't have the opportunity to slow down and mourn for a man who was at once both a father and a pastor to him. Leaving those feelings unaddressed creates the kind of debris that is going to eventually smack right into us and cause some damage. It was a while before he was able to have his own moments of grief without having them tied to responsibility.

We have to allow ourselves the time to cut the thrusters and attend to ourselves and our families. When I found out I needed to have surgery, I went to pastor, mentor, and friend, Dr. Alfred C. D. Vaughn, and told him about it. He wished me well and asked me what day I had scheduled the surgery. I had to tell him that I hadn't scheduled it because I just didn't have time. Too much was going on with the church and my family, and I couldn't break free. He looked at me in disbelief, then softened a little and finally said, "Well, then go ahead and die. If you don't have time to live, then go ahead and die." I was shocked at first, but then it hit me; I was being ridiculous and senseless. I scheduled the surgery that very day!

Subjective well-being is the study of how people evaluate their lives on a cognitive and emotional level. In other words, it defines our *happiness*. Those who have studied subjective well-being have made interesting observations about what underlies our overall life satisfaction. They have found that, while we do need to give attention to our professional lives, a significant percentage of our lives should be focused on other things, like emotional well-being and personal relationships. In fact, we would all do well to prioritize familial, personal, and emotional development, and then professional development, in that order. Simply put, we need to reverse our priorities. We need to understand where our happiness comes from and seek that out consistently. As people of faith, we already know that happiness, like our sense of self, comes from within and not without. It finds its genesis in the inner sanctum of our soul where God resides, where purpose lives and applauds our efforts and strengthens our esteem. To achieve that kind of introspection requires us to drop out of warp speed. We need to slow down and work on building our identity, **strengthening the thread** with our families not despite our families. We can still be the leaders we need to be without pushing ourselves past the point of breaking. Cut the engines, take a breath, and bring back a measure of simplicity, priority, and good sense into your life. There is still beauty in a sunrise, delight in walking with a child, and satisfaction in just holding hands and feeling the company of the committed. There is a calmness that speaks to our spirit and soul when we slow down enough to embrace it, a calmness within which we will find our way with the rest of the THREAD Principle back to the people we were meant to be. It is not how fast we live that matters, but how what matters slows us down, so that we take note of every one of those sunrises, walks, and hands held, and etch them in our memories. Heed the warning instead of letting it pass by. "When you travel at warp speed, you will have a warped life."

We need to understand where our happiness comes from and seek that out consistently.

BREAKOUT SESSION WITH BISHOP THOMAS:

Hanging On By a Thread: How to Slow Down and Enjoy Life

What are some activities that you do to slow down and relax? List them here, including how often you participate in them, what they mean to you, and how they help.

_____

_____

_____

_____

_____

_____

_____

_____

_____

_____

_____

_____

Have you ever had an "epiphany" moment in which you realized that you needed to slow down and give attention to yourself, to others, or to issues in your life that you could no longer ignore? If you have not yet experienced such a moment, talk about how you feel regarding your stress level compared to your ability to relax.

_____

_____

_____

_____

_____

_____

_____

_____

_____

_____

_____

_____

_____

_____

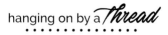

Talk about some parameters that you have recently placed on your life to manage stress and improve your quality of life. Or, talk about changes you need to make in your busy life. For the latter, talk about your plan to execute that idea.

_____

_____

_____

_____

_____

_____

_____

_____

_____

_____

_____

_____

_____

When you look back at your life, what moments stand out as deserving more attention than you gave them? How can you avoid warping through any more of those moments?

_____

_____

_____

_____

_____

_____

_____

_____

_____

_____

_____

_____

_____

CHAPTER **FIVE**

· ·

Harmonize Your Selves: Seeing and Understanding the Different Yous

So, you've found the time to slow down and take a breath. Now what? How do you get from the hectic, warped life you have now, with your families in distress and your lives off the path to self-actualization, and get back to where you saw yourself, where God wants you to be?

Let me answer that with another question: *What do you mean by "you"?*

What defines "you" as a person? Are you a leader or a family man or family woman first? Are you an American first? Are you a tennis- or golf-lover first? Perhaps, quite rightly, you'd put your worship of God first or define yourself by your church or community. But none of those completely encapsulates you, me, or any of us. We can't be summed up by a single quadrant of our lives. The human soul is much vaster and more diverse than that.

That abundance of diversity brings with it contradictory priorities and stress that we often struggle to harmonize if we are moving too quickly through life. The truth is, we are neither one nor another thing "first"; we are all things at all times. We live many different lives and have many different selves, and the only way to make all those disparate pieces work together is if we take that breath and then allow each piece to find its place in our complete, harmonious identity.

Yet, we always have something pushing against that impulse. Bishop T.D. Jakes, Senior Pastor of The Potter's House, a 30,000 member church and international outreach organization located in Dallas, TX, says that it is our instincts that lead us to discover our calling. We are drawn to our calling in business, family, community, and God by a primitive, subconscious force. That logic helps explain why some of us are so immersed in our work. As Jeremiah told us, God knew us before we were born. He called us to this life, and we answered.

It almost goes without saying that this truth leads us to hold ourselves to high standards in every aspect of our lives. It is in our nature as leaders and Christians to want to excel as professionals, family people, and people of faith. We represent the God of all creation. We claim to be God's representatives. It is because of that role that we are forced to look at ourselves critically and say, like Isaiah, *"'Woe to me!' I cried, 'I am ruined! For I am a man of unclean lips, and I live among a people of unclean lips, and my eyes have seen the King, the Lord Almighty'"* (Isaiah 6:5). We fall victim to the expectations we have of ourselves. As people who follow our calling to live a strong Christian life, we expect a certain level of perfection from ourselves; when we fall short, when we "fall to pieces," we can become our own worst enemies. We begin to judge and condemn our every action and initiative. We scrutinize and closely examine everything we do, and we question the outcome of every situation, no matter how hard we work or how good our intentions.

Part of this pressure comes from the fact that we know many people are aware of our skill level and what we consistently bring to the table. We understand that they expect this level of ability and commitment at all times. We have an *A-Game*, and they are expecting us to bring it. Unfortunately, they do not know what drives us, and they don't understand what sustains and invigorates us. Conversely, they don't know what drags us down and makes us weak. For us, the irony is that our drive to succeed in all areas of life is so great that when we take stock of our lives, the gaps in our "needs met" column are found not in our work and public performance, but in our private failures, our poor behavior, and our emotional distance. We all tend to live by a motto my mother told me once: "It's better to wear out than rust out." And wear out we do. And wear down, because the different pieces of our personalities rub up against each other, and like any engine, that causes friction if the pieces aren't put back into alignment. In order to avoid this, we need to get to know the different pieces of our lives and begin sorting them into their proper places.

FOUR DISTINCT LIVES

To begin with, to handle all our pressure, stress, and obligations, we divide ourselves into four distinct "lives"—professional, public, personal, and private. This is perfectly natural. In fact, everyone—busy or not, leader or not—does it. Most of us treat these lives differently, as if each is wholly unique and separate, as if each is our entire life *in toto* (in total). That, too, is perhaps healthy and normal up to a point, until we begin piling way too much into each life and expect them all to function properly. Instead of living each life as if it is our only life, we need to consider them as parts of a whole, taking note of how they affect each other. That way, we can better appreciate the part each has to play in our harmonized life. You are not just your job, your

church, or your family. You are all of those, and more. Each part needs to function with the others.

You are not just your job, your church, or your family. You are all of those, and more.

As leaders, we are probably most familiar with our **professional life**. This is the life in which we tend to feel we have the most control. We mark the boundaries of this life very carefully in order to maintain a semblance of competence no matter what is happening elsewhere in our other lives. Our professional life is the one where we hold meetings, negotiate business deals, interact with officials, manage employees, and in my case, preach the gospel. In the professional life, we know the rules of engagement in each arena and walk into every situation well-armed for whatever it may bring. We promote our church or business or social and bureaucratic family interests, and we make sure that we are doing the best for whatever unit or organization our professional side represents. We develop a well-run "machine" that oversees a number of activities, interacting with people within and outside our organization in countless ways. Above all, we know we are doing it all well. In our positions, we act as role models for everyone below, above, and around us. Whether we realize it or not, we all make a point of putting on our professional hat when the time comes and wearing it well. It is here that our intellect shines, our skills are honed, and our words are chosen appropriately. It is here that we hope and expect to succeed.

And those troubles only sum up the professional life we live. Our **public life** has its own problems. This is the life we are living when

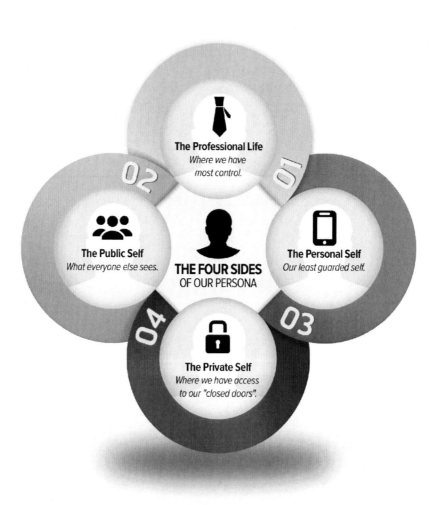

The Professional Life
Where we have most control.

The Public Self
What everyone else sees.

THE FOUR SIDES
OF OUR PERSONA

The Personal Self
Our least guarded self.

The Private Self
Where we have access to our "closed doors".

we walk down the street or through the mall. It's the side observed at the market when someone stops to chat. The public life is where we display our temperament, our attitude, and our love or disregard for the very people God sent us to serve and interact with. It is in this life that we must never forget that we are called to be servants as well as leaders. This is our life on display. We have to be there for acquaintances, neighbors, strangers, and the community. In short, we have to be there for everybody. Our public life is the one in which we are constantly visible and constantly sought out.

This openness to scrutiny is not always the easiest situation to handle. Our public life is not always a completely honest one. Some qualities have to be suppressed in order to put the right face forward for our neighbors. The struggle of wanting to be ourselves often clashes with this demand. I had to learn the hard way that people gain faith by seeing God, not by seeing a very human pastor; people come to us for help after observing us in the heat of the battles of life, not from hearing our sermons or witnessing our leadership style. One of the marks of the postmodern era is a rebellion against such demands. The cry goes up: "You have to take me as I am." As tempting a rebellion as it is, it just doesn't work for us as leaders, particularly Christians leaders. That professional life interferes with our desire for an open public face. We cannot forget that we are not called to just *do us*; we are called to *represent God*. The luxury of just being ourselves is denied to us, and while we are happy to make that sacrifice, it does cause strain.

In contrast to the regimented public life, our **personal life** is our least guarded, the version of life we sometimes wish we could make public. With this life, we bring people into the personal space in which we live.

Our personal life is the one in which we interact with our families and other close relationships. It is the freest life we have. This is the life that longs to be happy and seeks to move in that direction. Yet even here, we find many issues to contend with, including constant family dramas and crises. Friends may count on us for too much, and of course, we can't say "no" to anything. As leaders and doers, more is expected of us in terms of tolerance and giving, even in this sphere, and this can lead to the same old tensions of taking on too much. On top of that, our personal life doesn't always finesse its way through a problem or use the most neutral language to handle a crisis; it speaks its mind. This level of relationship intimacy offers us the opportunity to speak less cautiously and reveal our true feelings. Obviously, this can lead to some conflict. Even if we can manage to hold all that in place, even as we try to take refuge from our public selves, which are always on stage, we are still also trying to keep all our personal issues from spilling over into our other lives. We are running in two lanes at the same time. We struggle to keep our professional and public lives as the fixer and the doer from the open and unguarded person we are in personal time, but that is a tall order. There is no leader alive who at some point has not felt as if he or she would lose his or her mind from managing the two tensions. Still, most would admit, even our personal space does not grant us completely unguarded freedom. We are still cautious not to swing open all the doors even with the closest of friends.

That is where the **private life** comes in, the life only we have access to, where those closed doors are all thrown open, and where we often meet our greatest concerns. It almost seems as if we are walking down stairs into the quagmire of existence as we move from the insulated professional, to the public personification, to the personal struggler, and finally to the hidden person who lurks in the dark chambers of pain, fear, questions, and unresolved issues. On top of trying to handle all that is required in our professional lives AND maintaining an open and helpful face in the public AND dealing with the inevitable personal issues that everyone deals with, we also have to internalize and attempt to handle all that comes with being who we are privately. Considering the extra stress we have as leaders not to let too much of these internal struggles out, it is inevitable that our anger and disappointments will at some point rise up and flood this basement level of our person until we can hardly handle them. It is here that our unmet needs are hidden and suppressed. Here is where our dark side has been banished. This is the life that few have ever encountered. It is an intense and sometimes chaotic place, and there are times that it becomes far too much for any individual to handle. We have witnessed leaders caught in scandal innumerable times, in innumerable professions because their private lives have finally burst forth into public. Others grow so exhausted facing their demons, they commit suicide, unable to take the tension one more day. The reports of breakdowns and burnouts are not over-exaggerated. It takes so much energy to keep this life from breaking bad; it takes a constant struggle to keep the monster from breaking out of the cage.

It is only the grace of God that gives us the strength to keep the cage closed, to avoid becoming a casualty of our own drama. God has equipped us with His grace so that we can grow in the tension, through the tension, and because of the tension. I have learned to value that grace, rather than discount it. There is no amount of study that equips me for the power of the tensions that tear at our lives. The forces are cosmic and intend to be crippling, but God's grace gives us the strength of Samson to pull down the temple pillars, the wisdom of Paul to say, *"My power is made perfect in weakness"* (2 Cor. 12:9), and the assurance of Jesus that, *"surely I am with you always to the very end of the age"* (Matthew 28:20).

This grace is very much needed, because the private life is often like a sewer, sucking down all our dark thoughts from all our different lives and pooling below the surface. It is who we started out to be now deformed by what we have been through and could not handle. It is that part of us that wants to be loved into the light but can't find the door to let the light in. It is that life we are afraid to let come out and play. It is here that we internalize fears about our professional lives, internalize the anxiety of public scrutiny, and internalize the stress of keeping that personal sanctuary intact. All those internalized emotions have to go somewhere, so down the drain they go to our private lives. Some might say that their personal and private lives are one in the same, that they are so rigorously honest or that they hold no secrets below the surface when they are around those they trust. I would argue, however, that we must—and almost always do—keep them separate. They are two distinct aspects of our identity. Having a sewer in our various versions of ourselves is necessary and healthy if we keep it clean. We need this private space where we can contemplate our traumas without any fear of alienation or embarrassment. Even when we allow a reasonable number of people into our personal circles, we still need to restrict them from our private selves. We need to keep that section dominated by us and those trained to help us. To imagine what happens if we don't manage our private life upkeep, just think about what your house looks like when the pipes get clogged.

Those clogs and broken pipes are easier to come by than you might think. It is important to remember that the private life is a fragile and emotionally bare place. Here, we have all our insecurities and hurts tucked away; we keep our subconscious protected, and we hide the pain we have felt throughout life. Because we cannot bring ourselves to let all of our issues out in the light, we force them here to wrestle with in order to find answers and resolutions. But when we don't integrate our lives and let them work together to keep us healthy, when we force too much into our lives and put too much pressure on our professional and public lives, we end up flooding the basement with all the issues we have to hide away.

There's a limit to how much we can leave locked up in our emotional basement. If we let things pile up down there too long without addressing them, we run the risk of causing greater harm to ourselves. I used to find that whenever I was hurting and in the midst of great crisis—when I would retreat to the private centers of my mind—I would find my whole lifetime's worth of pain and past hurts down there waiting for me. Instead of it being a private place to wrestle out answers, it had become a storage vault for the years of suppressed feelings that had been forced out of my other lives. The place of my private refuge had become a place to view every failure and disappointment. It is here that we find our very heavy negative emotions, and it is here that the hurt can become unbearable. We have all had experiences that were heartbreaking and devastating. We have all been hurt to the core. We have all suffered from our own form of depression, and we have all buried many of the feelings associated with it in our private space. So long as we go down regularly, tidy up a bit, and work through these issues, these buried feelings are fine. If we don't, if we can't find the time because we are too busy with our other lives, our place for contemplation becomes the place where the emotions associated with our traumas reside. If we don't wander down and do some basic housekeeping, that region can become so overwhelming that we become afraid to be by ourselves for fear of the thoughts we will have to face.

The grace of God that is so powerfully released upon our lives is the only force that can redeem this broken private life and restore it to wholeness. We cannot keep suppressing and repressing. There comes a moment when we have to let the primal scream reach the heart and ears of God and let God minister to the brokenness that seeks to raise its head. That part of us is crying out for acceptance and redemption, and that is the work of God. As I will discuss more in the next chapter, God's grace can restore our broken lives and let the hurts and disappointments become integrated into our personhood. We become whole even as we know we have been hurt. It is at this level that we experience such a thankfulness to God that our lives now have a chance to be complete and whole.

A WINDOW TO OUR DIFFERENT SELVES

I don't think we realize just how complicated we are. We shy away from the conversations that give insight into our complicated nature. In fact, four lives in, we aren't even close to seeing the whole person who is staring back at us in the mirror. We aren't just the lives we live, we are also a series of different "selves" as well. I have found a tool that is useful to help people come to grips with how complex they are and how they are seen by others: the Johari Window, developed by and named after two American psychologists, Joseph Luftv and Harrington Ingham. The diagram is usually represented by four quadrants that speak directly to what we know about ourselves and what others know about us. The selves on the quadrants are:

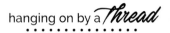
1. The Open Self, where information that we and others know about us resides

2. The Blind Self, where information that we do not know about ourselves but others know about us resides

3. The Hidden Self, where information that only we know about ourselves resides

4. The Unknown Self, where information about us that we and others know nothing about at all resides

To access and become more comfortable with these different selves, a person chooses from a series of adjectives to describe him or herself and then has colleagues or friends choose their own set of adjectives. The choices are then compared to see what qualities manifest in both the individual and the group, and which are seen by only one or the other. The result is a deeper appreciation of our multilayered personalities and an introduction to what we have tried and what we have succeeded in hiding about ourselves. By performing this exercise with others, it allows us to let people in and familiarize them with the struggles we have locked away in our private lives. It also makes us aware of how open or hidden we really are.

You do not necessarily have to go through the whole Johari Window exercise to gain these insights. Simply knowing that there are so many "selves" within us is enlightening to most of us; however, how many of us actually realize that there is a self that no one, not even we ourselves, know at all? How many fully understand that there is a self that others see, but we do not? These ideas can be mind-blowing, hard to understand, and even daunting and fear-inducing. They are heady concepts that are hard to digest, and to add insult to injury, we

The **Johari Window**

THE FOUR SELVES

KNOWN TO SELF   UNKNOWN TO SELF

KNOWN TO OTHERS

ARENA
The one you show to others.

BLIND SPOT
The one you aren't aware of.

UNKNOWN TO OTHERS

FAÇADE
The one that only you know.

UNKNOWN
The one unknown to all.

know that it is God who is orchestrating this inner struggle so that we can be fully human and fully alive.

We've already talked about the grace God has given us to deal with our deepest traumas. Now, we know that God knows our struggles and our dilemmas, that God knows every side of us—even our hidden sides—and yet God makes us work this all out on our own.

Of course, this is for our own good. He uses our struggles to help us become free from our inner tensions and discover the joy of freedom. By engaging in this struggle, by choosing to no longer ignore it, we are drawn closer to God. God wants us to harmonize our selves and our lives, to **strengthen the thread** instead of letting it fall to pieces in our hands. We have to acknowledge the good it does us to delve into what makes us tick and, ultimately, what will empower us to heal. We have to stop wrestling with a self that we can't handle alone, and we have to confront these hidden issues. Once we begin to associate God with the struggle, the hurt, and the healing, we are able to acknowledge that this process will ultimately work out for our good. As Romans 8:28 says, *"In all things God works for the good of those who love Him, who are called according to His purpose."*

There are so many layers to us (God has created these multiples), and so it is our responsibility as Christians to investigate them and learn to handle them. Knowing what we are up against helps when we are **hanging on by a thread**. It allows us to find our way back to a better, balanced life. This is why it is good to acknowledge and reference the Johari Window now and then. The key to overcoming the mess we've left in our private lives is to confront the pain and the insecurities that have been left unaddressed too long. We need to be brave enough to acknowledge our issues and trusting enough to let a few people in as we work towards healing. No one can do this alone, and herein lies the problem because *trust can be the biggest issue of all.*

We throw the word around a lot, but trust is built upon a firm foundation of *respect;* we only trust people who we feel *truly respect us.* Let me be clear: I am not talking about people we respect. I am talking about people we feel respect us. We can respect others because of their abilities, skills, or position, but that does not necessarily mean the respect is returned to us. They can ignore us when they are with others. They can betray our confidences. They can dismiss us like dew on a hot day. The respect I am speaking of causes us to value the relationship because we are valued. We really cannot trust people who do not respect or value us. We need to be confident that the people in our inner circles are those we can trust. There are countless individuals that will try to get close to us. Many times, our public personas will draw people who look up to us, but that is not the respect I'm talking about either. Respect is valuing others or having an inherent feeling that you do not want to see them hurt.

It may seem like an impossible task to find such people, but I do believe God puts people in all of our lives who we can trust to enter this space with us. Sometimes, it is a paid professional; other times, it is a special friend. The key is accepting the support and help of that person as we venture into the uncharted territory of personal, inner healing. There are not many people who will establish that kind of trust relationship with us, but there are always a few. Few people ever get to know the scared little child or the starved-for-love adult that resides deep in our hearts and minds. Our job is to find those few and let them in. It is essential to let light into the dark space we like to ignore and begin to allow ourselves to heal and live the life we have been given. God will bring true friends and helpers into our lives, much like Jonathan was to David, and they should be cherished. In my life, I have learned to be grateful for my inner circle of friends—albeit a small one by most people's standards, only a few friends and my wife—who have helped guide me through uncharted waters. I don't have to talk to them every day, but I know that they are there when I need them, and they know I am there for them when they need me.

We are not a single person to know but a vast series of people all coming together as one. We have to pay attention and work on all those different parts to make sure they are all working properly on their own and together as a unit. God has put everything into place for us, accounting for each separate life that we live and each separate self that we project into the world. We have witnessed God's guidance in calling us to our professional lives. We have tried to be a worthy face for God's benevolence in our public eyes. We have felt God's kindness and His love in the people He has allowed into our personal lives. We need to trust the connections God has provided for us to overcome our struggles in our private lives. Likewise, we know God is part of how we see ourselves, how others see us, and even, we must know deep down, a part of that self that no one but He knows. We are not any one of these lives or selves in whole, but we are all of them in part. Only by allowing God into every space and alcove of our divided person can we ever find the harmony that brings all of us together into one. God has provided this harmony, but we have to put our trust in God and others to receive it. And that is just what we will do in the next chapter.

We are not a single person to know but a vast series of people all coming together as one.

BREAKOUT SESSION WITH BISHOP THOMAS:

Hanging On By a Thread: Where Do You Go for Help with Private Issues?

List some of your closest friends and detail what they mean to you. Are they people you feel you can trust with your private life secrets?

_____

_____

_____

_____

_____

_____

_____

_____

_____

_____

_____

_____

_____

_____

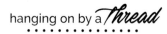

If you were to use the Johari Window, what qualities would you express about yourself? What qualities do you think others would see?

_____

_____

_____

_____

_____

_____

_____

_____

_____

_____

_____

_____

_____

_____

_____

Can you remember a time that you felt deeply hurt? How have you
healed or not healed in the time since this happened to you?

_____

_____

_____

_____

_____

_____

_____

_____

_____

_____

_____

_____

_____

_____

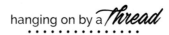

Can you remember one of the happiest times of your life? Detail that here or detail a scenario that you would like to see happen in your life. If you are feeling like a prolific writer today, detail both.

_____

_____

_____

_____

_____

_____

_____

_____

_____

_____

_____

_____

_____

_____

CHAPTER **SIX**

• •

Reinvest in God: How David and Paul Show You the Way Forward

When I offer advice to people about getting their lives back on track, I often use the language of finance. Imagine yourself as an investment banker, I tell them, looking to make optimal profits off yourself. In order to get the most for your money, you don't invest once in one area and walk away. Instead, you have to be willing to pull your money out when the market changes and put it in a better, more productive area. The same holds true for your happiness. To find balance and fulfillment in life, you have to be willing to become an expert at what I like to call "de-investing" and "re-investing."

As I mentioned in chapter three, the anchoring point in the THREAD Principle, the main currency that we work in, is our belief in God. Though every step in the process is important, the whole thread falls apart if we don't have God there strengthening every fiber. For our own mental, spiritual, and even physical health, then, it is vitally important for us not to put off reorganizing all the investments of our various selves around God. We need to learn to pull out of bad investments that do not add any value to our lives, and put our emotional capital elsewhere.

"The Serenity Prayer" attributed to Reinhold Neibuhr says it best: *"God, grant me the serenity to accept the things I cannot change, the courage to change the things I can, and the wisdom to know the difference."* This is the essence of spiritual investing: knowing where we must remain invested, where we should de-invest, and where we should re-invest again. As obvious as that might seem, it can be a difficult concept to accept. We don't always consider the fact that we need to re-invest in ourselves regularly. Once we settle on one path or one outlook, we tend to stick with it, no matter how much our stock goes down. Even though new self-investment is healthy and actually makes us more productive and fulfilled, we still pretend our old choices are big winners and there's no reason to rethink the investment portfolio, no matter what opportunities arise.

As you can probably guess, our bad investments stem from denial. We are in denial about so many things, such as what we need, where we should be focusing our energies, and what we should really be doing with our lives. This denial runs counter not just to our own needs, but to our calling as Christians. God wants us to be invested in the process of self-actualization, in the search for wholeness and fulfillment, even if it is discovered traveling a rocky road. As Paul says in Romans 12:2, *"Do not conform to the pattern of this world, but be transformed by the renewing of your mind. Then you will be able to test and approve what God's will is—his good, pleasing and perfect will."* That is why we must come to grips with the areas of our lives that are out of sorts. We need to pull out of our bad investments to de-invest in the things that are not adding to our search for self-actualization, and are in fact taking us from it. Then, we need to re-invest that time and attention to discovering and cultivating our authentic selves. Only once we have found this true self can we become who God has designed us to become.

While finding our way to this truth can be painful, the relief it offers far outweighs the cost. It is only in the truth of God that the scattered and divided pieces of our personality can come together as a harmonious whole. Over the years, I have found that when I accept this truth about myself, I am released from much of the pain that held me down because I allowed it to—whether the pain was caused by poor decisions, difficult situations, or the things I wanted to change about myself. This truth becomes a battering ram demolishing the debtor's prison that holds us captive. In these moments of letting go, I feel freedom, and at the same time and in equal measure, I feel that I begin to know Jesus more deeply because I have really let Him in and trusted Him to be my guide. When I let go, I allow Him to bring a transformation into my life. I understand and appreciate the freedom, the productivity, and the renewed sense of success that letting go allows. I finally understand what Paul meant in Galatians 5:1 when he wrote: *"It is for freedom that Christ has set us free."*

And, it is for this reason that David is one of my heroes.

Psalm 23

A psalm of David.

1 The LORD is my shepherd, I lack nothing.

2 He makes me lie down in green pastures,
he leads me beside quiet waters,

3 he refreshes my soul.
He guides me along the right paths
for his name's sake.

4 Even though I walk
through the darkest valley,

I will fear no evil,
for you are with me;
your rod and your staff,
they comfort me.

5 You prepare a table before me
in the presence of my enemies.
You anoint my head with oil;
my cup overflows.

6 Surely your goodness and love will follow me
all the days of my life,
and I will dwell in the house of the LORD
forever.

These words are well-known and well-loved, yet their context is often missing when we consider them. David is not the shepherd; he did not call the Lord "his shepherd" when he was himself a shepherd, watching sheep on the backside of the Judean hills. They are not the musings of a lad under the stars. No, they are the words of a king; the words he found courage to utter only when his life was in shambles, when he was forced to leave his home because his son sought his life. The accumulation of bad family decisions, the weight of ruling, and the inherent insecurity the shepherd had in being king did not always allow him to know the best of himself. Indeed, as we all know, he often ran away from his best self to catastrophic results. Yet, in that season, he claimed the power that would enable him to reclaim the throne.

Our denial of our needs and refusal to change can sometimes threaten our ability to manage ourselves, even in a crisis. David was almost in that position. The scent of failure was in the air and even his troops wondered about the great man they knew as king. However, at that moment, David re-invested himself in his relationship with God, pleading for guidance "along the right paths." That choice gave him the power to rise to the challenge presented to him. When David left his home, he was **hanging on by a thread**, but by the end of the story, he changed his investment strategy and invested heavily in his relationship with God and honesty with himself, allowing him to rise back to glory.

Our denial of our needs and refusal to change can sometimes threaten our ability to manage ourselves, even in a crisis.

It was not always clear that David would show such wisdom. As a boy, a soldier, and a king, he successfully overcame many struggles, but he did not always shine as a sterling example of a moral leader. We get to know David through his mistakes and the myriad crises in which he found himself embroiled. And through our thorough examination of this painstakingly human man, we discover that we all live David's story. We all make mistakes while trying to put ourselves in the way of happiness and success. Many times, like David, we just don't realize the consequences of our actions; we feel a need for more from life, as well as a sense of stress and disappointment that leads us to seek solace in poor choices. We make these poor choices because we refuse to look at ourselves honestly enough to make healthy changes. We may have the admiration of many, but for this very reason, we internalize or outright run away from our feelings because we think they may make us seem weak, or worse, vulnerable. We know that we are in our darkest valley, but we forget to let God be our rod and staff to guide us to truth. We are hurting and close to breaking, but we still refuse to cast aside our denial. Instead, we put more pressure on ourselves and demand more when we have no more to give. The sad truth is that, for some of us, this is the only life we know. We have never fully discovered inner peace or inner satisfaction. At best, we get a glimpse of it now and then. And by constantly living in moments of worry and desperation, like David, we can make bad decisions that impact others and send us stumbling down the road of additional bad decisions and ensuing consequences.

> *We may have the admiration of many, but for this very reason, we internalize or outright run away from our feelings because we think they may make us seem weak, or worse, vulnerable.*

David's story is filled with attempts to find inner peace that were costly to others. He was, after all, a man out of place, a man searching for direction in a life foreign to his background. He was an outsider to palace life, but a dweller within its walls, which gave him internal insecurities and external challenges. He was imprisoned by his position and could do little about his turmoil. On more than one occasion, his spirit cried out. The Psalms contain pages from his diary, and the messages let us know the depth of his inner conflict. He cried out about his sin. He acknowledged his desire to escape the weight of his work. He prayed for inner peace. Any leader can appreciate the burden that was on the poor shepherd's shoulders.

I don't think we realize how much energy David expended—that we also expend every day—trying to stay afloat, trying to keep the warring parts of his personality in check. In trying to keep our various lives in balance and spare others from pain, we make decisions that are not always in our best interest or even the best interest of those we love. We allow the flesh to win over our spirit, and that can have terrible consequences. It can reduce our sense of self-esteem and self-worth, it can tear apart the seams of purposeful relationships, and it can lead us into self-destructive paths from which recovery is extremely difficult. When we refuse to directly confront the overwhelming stressors we are facing, we can set in motion a series of events that can have devastating consequences. Just like David, we all fall prey to this dynamic. We try to remain strong, but what we consider strength is actually obstinacy from facing ourselves and our struggles. The Holy Spirit has been given to us to be our counselor and guide. The Spirit is sent to enable us to get a grip and re-invest in the power of the kingdom. We need to start listening to the Spirit and start double-checking our choices instead of doubling down on them.

David learned that lesson. When he cried out for God's *"goodness and mercy (or love)"* in Psalm 23, he made the choice to commit to God's wisdom instead of his own attempts to obfuscate his poor choices. What followed was a tragic but necessary victory, a restoration of his crown, and a true and powerful admission of his feelings in public. It was only by opening himself up to this path that he could restore his life to some semblance of its proper purpose. Though the path was painful, David took it, and God gave him the strength to complete it.

In my own life, I preach to others to turn away from denial and find their truth—what really makes them fulfilled. When I preach these ideas, I believe, as all pastors do, that my congregation is listening. We all feel this way, that we know enough to counsel others in our roles as leaders. But we are often trying so hard to earn that privilege as a prophetic voice that we overwhelm ourselves with a desire to be perfect: to be the perfect pastor, the perfect employee, the perfect parent, the perfect student. And by forcing ourselves down that road—one no man or woman can possibly succeed on—we refuse to see what we need to change in ourselves.

In my own life, I preach to others to turn away from denial and find their truth—what really makes them fulfilled.

Early in my career, I was no different. While I was talking about living as an individual in Christ, I felt that I had to be the embodiment of all the best virtues in a Christian. I became a pastor at age twenty-five. I was the youngster among the adults. I felt like little David, called upon to strike down Goliath. I had to prove something. I had to be capable. I had to be competent. I had to be professional. I had to be spiritual. I had to have all the gifts and graces in their fullness. I worked at being the best, feeling that my best was just making me adequate. My peers were seasoned saints, and they knew what a pastor should be like. I was young in my first role, and I was trying to measure up. I did as most new pastors do: I lost myself in the work, trying to live up to others' expectations and thereby earning their approbation. At the beginning of my career, I sought to appear relevant to the older members. Now, I am aware I can get caught trying to appear relevant to the younger generation. We all do this in our various positions. We all try to accommodate everybody and often feel as if we are losing ourselves in the effort as we leave our own needs behind, ignoring our own advice and failing to de-invest and re-invest in ourselves. Yes, this self-denial does *feel* right; it *feels* like we are doing well, but we are failing ourselves, just as David often failed himself and those close to him.

Returning to Paul—a man who knew something about taking a hard look and reinvesting in God—Philippians 4:6-7 began to have new meaning for me when I realized this. *"'Do not be anxious about anything,' he says, 'but in every situation, by prayer and petition, with thanksgiving, present your requests to God. And the peace of God, which transcends all understanding, will guard your hearts and your minds in Christ Jesus.'"* This anxiety Paul talked about comes from our denial of our different selves. Denial is so destructive because it causes us to invest in a future we don't want to experience. Exchange denial for truth, and see a future and an outcome that will take you to a new level. It is an act of will. It is a decision we have to make. It is not a one-time decision; it is a daily decision, hourly decision, moment-by-moment decision. In every instant, we must choose to see ourselves where we are at peace—productive and proud enough to declare: "This is the will of God concerning me in the circumstance in which I find myself!"

Exchange denial for truth, and see a future and an outcome that will take you to a new level.

In life, choices that were once positive can turn intolerable. It is a rite of passage to experience the slowing of currents in a once strong and dynamic relationship or to feel the lull of boredom in what was once an intriguing job or profession. In these cases, we don't do ourselves or anyone else any good when we allow the situation to persist. We must make a re-investment. As I've shared previously, at one time in my life, my young, child-free, untethered self thought that traveling and networking were what I needed to be fulfilled. However, my middle-aged father, husband, and provider self found that missing my kids' activities or missing family dinners to continue my old networking goals did not work for me anymore. It took a long time to admit to myself that I had to de-invest in one area and re-invest in another, but eventually I did it.

The failure to recognize this need to change our investments can lead to a lot of negative emotional consequences. Anger and resentment can build up over the years. Negative feelings facilitate other deeper issues, causing us to isolate ourselves emotionally and even physically from others. I have encountered many people from all walks of life who have nearly succumbed to the feeling of despair. Many know the voice of despair. The news reminds us that there are people who will sit up late at night and think about a world that is better without them, then get up the next day, put on a happy face, and continue on the same path as before. This is a dangerous practice.

It is with these people in mind that we must learn from David and Paul and give ourselves up to God and His plan for us. When we redirect our energies toward de-investing in what is pulling the pieces of our personality apart and re-invest in the person we have become in Christ, we develop within ourselves the strength to embrace the blessing of change. There comes a moment when we can break free from the inner prison that holds captive such potential. When we put our lives in God's hands and commit to becoming free, a transformation ensues. De-investing and re-investing is not easy. It is difficult work. The goal, however, is to be whole and to be fulfilled. It is worth taking a chance for such a goal with such a God. It is OK to admit that, like David, we are human and that we, too, have family problems and professional and personal issues. We, too, feel lonely and need help. We, too, walk through our darkest valley and need our shepherd. God is there for us; God will always be there for us. He knows when we are hurting, and He honors our attempts to right our lives. When we make the decision to let go of the things that do not add value to our lives, invest in the things that do, and trust God fully, we are finally ready to reach out, to extend ourselves into the new territory we have needed to walk in but have been afraid to go to. Once we have invested in getting God on our side, we are ready to find our place for change between comfort and fear.

It is OK to admit that, like David, we are human and that we, too, have family problems and professional and personal issues.

BREAKOUT SESSION WITH BISHOP THOMAS:

Hanging On By a Thread: Updating Your Investment Portfolio

List some areas you should de-invest in in your life. Where would you re-invest this energy? Try to address all areas: emotional, spiritual, physical, etc... Detail why the old investments no longer add value to your life and how the new investments will bring you new fulfillment.

_____

_____

_____

_____

_____

_____

_____

_____

_____

_____

_____

_____

_____

In your life, when have you called out to God for guidance when you were lost? Again, try to tap all areas of life and detail why these issues cause you pain.

_____

_____

_____

_____

_____

_____

_____

_____

_____

_____

_____

_____

_____

_____

In your own words, write a short paragraph about what makes you happy. Contrast this with what your younger self would have said. Have you remained true to yourself and your needs or do you remain tethered to your old path?

_____

_____

_____

_____

_____

_____

_____

_____

_____

_____

_____

_____

_____

In your own words, compose a short paragraph talking about how your denial of your needs has caused pain or stress to yourself and to others in your life. Close this paragraph with how you might improve on these negative parts of your life.

_____

_____

_____

_____

_____

_____

_____

_____

_____

_____

_____

_____

_____

_____

CHAPTER **SEVEN**

· ·

Extend Yourself: Finding a Place for Change Between Your Comfort and Fear Zones

"Change or die!" That's what my pastor friend, Dr. Vaughn, told me many years ago in that life-saving conversation in which he convinced me to schedule my surgery. His words became a big part of my awakening and my plans to change. I was a young man at the time, one who thought he was too busy and too important to deal with his health crisis, one who was so set in his ways he wouldn't break routine and extend himself out of his comfort zone even if it meant serious consequences to his health. I remember being taken aback by his comment. What was this man telling me? In very few words, his message was clear: I was so enmeshed in my obligations to my ministry that I couldn't see my own life clearly, couldn't change direction no matter the cost. I can tell you, the message got through to me quite quickly—right there, in fact.

Regardless of what I wanted from that conversation, I did not expect Dr. Vaughn to look me in the eye and tell me to change or die without even clarifying the meaning of his comment. Truthfully, he didn't need to anyway. Once the words were out, I knew I was heading for personal destruction by ignoring my own health and my own needs; it just took an outside perspective to make me see it.

It took much longer to realize that I needed to extend myself and make changes in other areas of my life, though. It wasn't just a matter of scheduling the surgery; I still had to realize that I needed to make real changes in my life—no matter how scary they seemed—in order to continue to be effective in ministry, as well as in my family and personal life. For me, the lack of focus on priorities that were important to me was causing strife in my life that I had not yet acknowledged. For many, this simple oversight can manifest in extreme materialism or narcissism, both of which are very serious issues in any Christian's life.

As we continue into the second half of the THREAD Principle, this refusal to face the personal difficulties right in front of us will increasingly become our greatest battle. We have, by now, found the time to take a breath, to confront the various deficiencies in our different selves, and turned to God for help, but none of that will come to anything if we don't learn to extend ourselves into the uncomfortable world of change. Those of us in leadership positions tend to ignore any issues that arise and appear like they could be a detriment to our carefully manufactured emotional, spiritual, and/or physical stability. We see addressing such issues or even slowing down for such issues as a weakness. We also view extending ourselves out of our realms of command and expertise as a possible threat to our effectiveness and our ability to be the leaders we see ourselves as. Written out plainly, it's easy to see that this is nonsense. Not only are we trying to wish away issues that aren't going anywhere, we are denying ourselves the chance to heal. Yet, the very thing that is a threat to our sense of emotional well-being is also a wake-up call regarding changes that need to be made in our lives.

We have, by now, found the time to take a breath, to confront the various deficiencies in our different selves, and turned to God for help, but none of that will come to anything if we don't learn to extend ourselves into the uncomfortable world of change.

That insistence on change is the imperative we fear most of all. Change scares us. But change is precisely what we most need.

For many of us, our calling set the direction and plan for us in life, and we have stayed that course ever since. What if, however, our call was initially misinterpreted by our younger selves to be static and not dynamic? What if our call actually evolves? What if we are meant to move on at some time in our lives and discover new things? What if God really wants to use us to do new things, to open new doors, and to build upon the work of prior years? And what if we are limiting ourselves by becoming so enmeshed in our current situations that we can't move away from our set course even an inch? This doesn't mean you have to drop your calling and take on a whole new life. But ask yourself this: What if you are meant to expand the work over time and not just remain the same?

We have to trust that we can make this change happen. We have to practice some of that trust in God's plan we developed in the last chapter and allow our lives to unfold in increments as the years pass by and as we grow. God didn't make us perfect at twenty. He wanted us to extend ourselves beyond who we were then. Proverbs 3:5-6 says, *"Trust in the Lord with all your heart, and lean not on your own understanding; in all your ways submit to Him, and He will make your paths straight."* If God is telling us to extend in a new direction, we need to submit to His will. Confining ourselves to a single position in life undeniably adds immense stress; it makes our lives claustrophobic, especially when we feel the tug in our spirit to grow, to change, and to extend. Many times, we can't even breathe. As we continue to find success and move up into positions of leadership, we restrict ourselves even more as we are more and more often looked to for everything and by everybody. That kind of responsibility can make us feel there is no escape, no matter the reservations we may secretly have. We have to be omnipresent to the people in our businesses or congregations. We are relied upon for so many things that it is hard to even contemplate establishing new relationships or starting new endeavors. We are so deeply invested in the daily operations of our work that we don't allow ourselves to break away. Yet it is that same pull upon us that is calling us to make the changes we know are necessary.

At the root of a lot of dissatisfaction in our lives is the fact that we ignore the urgings of God and our own instincts, especially when they may insist we walk away from a familiar routine or transition into a new one. We push aside all of the analysis of our decisions, and we fail to recalibrate our priorities, a requirement of people in leadership roles. What have we done? What needs are we not fulfilling? Should we move on? Should we try something different? Once we've taken a breath and stopped to answer these questions, we will know it is time to expand our horizons. It's time to stop ignoring our own good sense due to the comfort we find in the regularity of our struggles or the fear of possible change. We know that, in the words of Moses in Deuteronomy 2:3, *"You have made your way around this hill country long enough."* It's time to face that command from God and from ourselves. No longer can we ignore its guidance and decide to take yet another turn around the hill.

> *Once we've taken a breath and stopped to answer these questions, we will know it is time to expand our horizons.*

To understand why we have ignored the command to extend ourselves and make the changes that are best for us, we need to think of our lives as existing between two basic zones. The first is our familiar *"Comfort Zone,"* which is the domain of routine, schedules, and the known. It is where we stay when things are going well but also where we stay to avoid the challenges and unease of pursuing the new. In short, it is the place we have lingered far too long. The new way forward is to be found in the other zone, our *"Fear Zone,"* a realm that we strive to minimize our time in. We avoid the Fear Zone with comfortable daily routines or by returning to emotional or physical space that is familiar even if it is also mundane and stress-inducing in its own right. In the Fear Zone, we find our deep desires and beyond-the-horizon dreams, as well as the unknown consequences of grand decisions and our secret potential that we dare not spend too much time searching for. It is that region where we see the statement of Jesus looking us in the eye reminding us that we *"will do even greater things than these"* (John 14:12). Like the disciples, we are afraid of the

THE **COMFORT** ZONE
OUR DAILY ROUTINES,
NETWORK OF PEOPLE,
& CURRENT PROFESSIONAL GOALS.

GROWTH & MOVEMENT.
LEAVING THE PAST BEHIND.

THE **FEAR** ZONE
NEW EXPERIENCES,
SPIRITUAL GROWTH,
& EXPANDED CIRCLE OF ACQUAINTANCES.

failure that might accompany trying. In other words, this is a place of great possibility, *but also great risk*. It's a place we pull back from even if we make a token effort to push the envelope a bit and venture out to test the waters in a different career or calling. Even if we seriously consider life in a different city or on a different path, we often just retreat back into the Comfort Zone, where the cost of action is so much less. This is a natural instinct; humans don't like to leave the comfort of a settled and secure space. The frontier is as dangerous as it is exciting. Those in leadership roles are especially vulnerable to this consideration because we often feel that so much of what other people rely on for daily comfort rests on our shoulders. It often takes the force of outside events to demand we take the steps away from comfort that we ought to take on our own.

Like the disciples, we are afraid of the failure that might accompany trying.

These lessons are not always easily or quickly learned, least of all by me. You would have thought that I would have learned from my pivotal epiphany with Dr. Vaughn, but I did not. Often, a lesson doesn't stick until we have exhausted our fortitude and our ability to adapt to the situation before us. Which is exactly what I did. I overcame my health struggles, and I simply expected life to return to normal from there. I was ready to return to my Comfort Zone, but other concerns were quick to arise. While I had learned how to step away from my routine to address my own overt health issues, I had not learned how to deal with being blindsided by the reality that something could happen to my wife and family that I could not fix. I had not learned that my bedrock, my church, could be forced into serious changes. But so it was. Shortly after my surgery, my wife had to have surgery. On top of that, there was the big move our church had made. I knew that my newer, bigger church faced larger mortgage bills, and my congregation had greater demands. I felt that I had moved forward, but I did so with a bit of a limp. I was crippled by a sense of my own mortality and my own limitations. Finally, all these events conspired to make me leave my Comfort Zone far in the rearview mirror and get me moving full-speed ahead into my Fear Zone.

I was forced to enter the Fear Zone and move my life in a different, unknown direction, but I am grateful now for what I learned there. It was in my Fear Zone that I discovered I could be the support that my family needed and they could be mine, and with that revelation, I discovered so much more about myself. I was able to cancel so much and make my family more important in my life. Seeing the satisfaction in their eyes became the impetus for me to be there for them even more. And the rejuvenation that took place in my family allowed me to find greater focus and purpose with my church. Thus, it was in the Fear Zone that I discovered where my long-lost priorities lie, and also where my happiness had been hiding dormant. While I felt happy and knew that at one point I had always kept happiness sacred, it no longer felt part of my everyday life. That is, until I tapped into the other areas of my psyche that had gone previously unexplored.

In her book, *The How of Happiness: A Scientific Approach to Getting the Life You Want*, Dr. Sonja Lyubomirsky, an author and professor in the Psychology Department at the University of California, Riverside, theorizes that we are all born with an inherent "baseline happiness" or a "happiness set point" to which we return after important positive or negative events. With the happiness set point, 50% of our happiness level is already set and only 10% is contingent on our situations and circumstances. This is why feeding our materialistic urges offers us a brief high, but one we can never sustain. A new car will lift us, new jewelry or a new wardrobe will excite us, and a lavish holiday will relax us, but none of this is long-lasting. In time, we all settle back into our happiness set points.

Of course, that is not the end of the story when it comes to happiness. Basic math tells us that an interesting percentage is still outstanding. In fact, 40% is left over from the above analysis. According to Dr. Lyubomirsky's theory, that 40% represents happiness that is completely under our control. Our own actions, behaviors, choices, and chosen outlook give us the opportunity to increase our happiness significantly and certainly outweigh the measly 10% afforded to temporary positive and negative events that offset our "set point." Pete Scazzero, who we've already met in this book, once said, "We have Jesus in our heart, but Grandpa in our bones." This means that we are genetically predisposed to a certain level of happiness, but our spirituality and daily choices can contribute significantly to that happiness. If we are predisposed to a low level of happiness, then we especially need to tap into what makes us happy outside those parameters, and that is not always easy.

To gain that power over our happiness, we need to **strengthen the thread** that connects us to it by stepping beyond the limits of our Comfort Zones. As I mentioned above, it was only when I was forced to re-examine my priorities, scary as that was, that I saw how much I was leaving unfulfilled in myself. Our Fear Zones hold many of our dreams and much of our happiness potential. This doesn't mean we

should jump right into the center of the Fear Zone and never look back. Recklessness is unlikely to bring us any closer to the person we want to be than being changed to old comforts. We still need that routine, that steadiness we've perfected. What we have to do is learn to live between the two zones. It is only in this middle area that we can both exist in our normal lives and also take the chances we need in order to change, leading to fulfillment and happiness.

To gain that power over our happiness, we need to **strengthen the thread** *that connects us to it by stepping beyond the limits of our Comfort Zones.*

This middle way calls out to us with real urgency. As pastors, businesspeople, parents, and community leaders, we know that many of our peers harbor deep unhappiness. Understanding that our own willingness to straddle these two zones can bring us out of our own periods of unhappiness can be a game-changer. Positive changes that indulge our healthy and normal interests can bring us back from the brink of paralyzing despair. It was like this for me. Only by stepping away from comfort could I reprioritize and realize that satisfaction in my life required more than the status quo with my family and my church.

Managing our inner lives to allow ourselves to take tentative steps into our Fear Zones and focus on new experiences and positive decisions can be the difference between changing and dying inside. We have to be careful, however, that we are not dying over what we don't have and only living when we get what we think we want. Those deep-seated dreams in our Fear Zones shouldn't be about cars or lavish trips; we've already talked about how temporary those things are. Instead, we must strive to fill the voids in our lives by making sure that we are focused on what is truly important to us. Family always has to remain a priority, as does our professional life, and above all, God. I hear the command of Jesus to *"seek first His kingdom and His righteousness, and all these things will be given to you."* (Matthew 6:33). We must always be willing to search deeper and examine how we live, whether we are exposing ourselves to negativity or allowing stress to get the best of us. It is those high and noble values and virtues that call us in the Fear Zone and allow us to see ourselves through the eye of greater purpose and meaningful living.

Of course, that is sometimes easier said than done. That is why, as we look to **strengthen the thread** further, we must next turn not inward but outward and look to others for help and advice.

We must always be willing to search deeper and examine how we live, whether we are exposing ourselves to negativity or allowing stress to get the best of us.

BREAKOUT SESSION WITH BISHOP THOMAS:

Hanging On By a Thread: How to Turn the Negative to Positive

What are some of the situations that have pushed you out of your Comfort Zone? List them here and explain what you learned from the experience.

_____

_____

_____

_____

_____

_____

_____

_____

_____

_____

_____

_____

_____

What do you think would bring you innate happiness? How have you taken steps to get to that point?

_____

_____

_____

_____

_____

_____

_____

_____

_____

_____

_____

_____

_____

_____

What parts of your life are you not making enough of a priority at the moment? How can you bring focus back to where your priority belongs?

_____

_____

_____

_____

_____

_____

_____

_____

_____

_____

_____

_____

_____

_____

When is the last time you tried to fix your deeper issues with an easy purchase? Detail how you felt afterward. How long was it before your issues returned?

_____

_____

_____

_____

_____

_____

_____

_____

_____

_____

_____

_____

_____

_____

_____

CHAPTER **EIGHT**

● ● ● ● ● ● ● ● ● ● ● ● ● ● ● ● ● ● ● ●

Accept Advice and Help:
Building Support Systems
for the Discovery Ahead

Once we have finally found the strength to extend ourselves into that space between comfort and fear so we can begin to discover who we are today, we have really stepped into the unknown. At such times, we leaders may want to simply forge ahead alone at this point, to show our strength and independence by taking on change on our own, but we all know that stepping out into the dark without a map means we will need a guide. We will need a helping hand. We will need support and advice.

But advice is tricky. My mother used to always say, "Advice is like quinine—easy to give, but hard to take." Quinine is great at treating a number of maladies, but it is a bitter liquid to swallow. So is advice. This holds true for our everyday advice from coaches, therapists, counselors, mentors, and friends, and it is all the more true when we consider advice from a higher source. When God is the one telling us where to go and how to change, we somehow grow all the more stubborn, even when stubbornness just keeps us further from the person we need to become and further from Him.

As a pastor, when I preach what I think is a life-changing Gospel to people each Sunday, I fully expect them to see and experience the result of this encounter with Jesus. For a long while, I just assumed that I, too, would feel the Gospel deeply, considering I was the one preaching to others. However, many times I, the messenger, felt as if the message had passed me by. Pastors can get so busy giving guidance, we forget to stop and absorb the message ourselves. Despite being in the business of dispensing the best advice ever given to man, I know I have to make the conscious effort to take the advice myself. Often, my fellow pastors and I are slow to realize that we may need to reaffirm God's Word in our lives and truly understand the power of our own individual faith.

This is not unique to pastors. These moments in which we find ourselves a bit lost as we pursue a new identity through THREAD can affect any of us. As leaders, we are by nature too enmeshed in our roles, whether that is imparting advice and strategy to employees or imparting the Word to a congregation. We become so focused on making sure that others are on the right track that we forget to check on ourselves. When I am asked how I define my mission, I say, "I am called to help people understand the meaning of faith in their lives and the will of God for their lives in the context in which they find themselves." We all need someone like that in our lives, someone there to help us reinvest in God and extend ourselves based off the context we find ourselves in today.

Jesus laid it all out for us when He looked at those who followed Him and directly said, *"Then you will know the truth, and the truth will set you free"* (John 8:32). Over the years, there have been times that I have not felt that freedom because I was not living my truth. In those times, when I was **hanging on by a thread**, I had wandered too far from the person I needed to be, and to find my way back again, I had to find the support to make changes in my life and reassess what I truly wanted. I had to find people who could give me that bitter advice that would lead me back to God, no matter how far outside my Comfort Zone He was.

We need to come to terms with the fact that today, in all areas of life, we are faced with far more diverse and constant challenges than previous generations. The enormity of what we deal with on a daily basis can bring anyone on any day down. It is hard to keep up and hard to stay positive in a world with a fluctuating economy and a fast-paced modern life. Let's face it, given the enormity of our jobs as workers and professionals, family leaders, and community leaders, we literally need a support team 24/7. If we don't put a support system in place, we will inevitably come up against the wall that we just don't have the skill set to handle. We have to leave time so we can take a breath and work through THREAD before we can press for even higher heights in our careers or social standings. But how can we gain that time without others to help relieve the pressure we are under?

We need to come to terms with the fact that today, in all areas of life, we are faced with far more diverse and constant challenges than previous generations.

None of us can be prepared for absolutely everything that life throws our way. We have to find places to go for help and give more attention to creating a support system that will sustain our needs. To create that support, we need to find people who know what we need, people who are ready to accept our fears, our hopes, our weaknesses, and our strengths.

The benefits of this go beyond our mental, spiritual, and physical health. We are better leaders when we are not overtaxed. The saying goes, when someone takes on too much in life, he or she is a "jack of all trades but a master at none." We have hidden potential in ourselves and in others that could be uncovered should we stop spreading ourselves so thin. If we channel our needs and our strengths into what we truly want out of life, we can be true masters at what we want to do. We can conquer what we want to in our lives. If we continue to maintain sole responsibility for our emotional state on top of everything else we supervise, making ourselves increasingly stressed and unhappy, then we will never find what we need. However, if delegated a little— passing off responsibilities both at work and personally that we can't handle alone—we will find the time to focus on who we are and who we are equipped to be. We will be able to make it through the crisis moments of life and see the role each crossroad plays in our lives.

> *If we channel our needs and our strengths into what we truly want out of life, we can be true masters at what we want to do.*

Dirty Harry, one of the great movie characters and philosophers of our pop culture world, said, "A man's got to know his limitations." This is so very true. Most of us can name the boundaries of our responsibilities outright—finances, sales pitches, preaching, running companies, tending to children, managing family and friends, staying healthy, public appearances, networking, community service, maintaining justice. That's quite a list of roles we are expected to take on, and we are sure to fall short in any number of them, especially if we try to take them all on at once. And this is hardly an exhaustive list; I am sure I left off plenty. Where are we going to find time, with all those responsibilities, to take care of ourselves? Where are we going to find the time to harmonize our different selves, to reinvest in God, and find the strength to extend ourselves into new areas?

Take another look at that long list of responsibilities. If we take the time to sit down and take stock of our lives, we might find that it is best to hire or consult with someone on our finances or sales and get that off our plates. We may decide that excessive travel for networking and public appearances is no longer important. We might decide that starting to eat better and beginning an exercise program might be in our best interests, and we should emphasize that at the expense of running the company singlehandedly. All of that will help, but it leaves out the area we most need support in: easing those emotional troubles that are less easy to innumerate. That proves a far more difficult task. To do that, we would need to reach out to others and tell them—at work, at home, in church—that we need help. We would need to seek professional assistance in sorting through our issues. Men are sometimes afraid to consult professionals, but these professionals can help us sort through the mix of emotions, issues, and even pathologies that are holding us hostage. We might need to ask for more of that bitter advice, and ask for more time to swallow it.

We need this support so we can continue to struggle for this truth. If we allow ourselves to avoid introspection and truly knowing ourselves, we cannot be free. If we refuse to seek out help and assistance, we pronounce a new restrictive sentence on our lives daily. We must all fight to reach this self-truth—this honest faith—and pastors are no exception. Over the years, I have had to revisit my understanding of the will of God, of the advice His Word is laying out for me. Questions presented themselves that made me wonder if I was even in the right profession. There were times I wondered if there were other things I needed to do. Such contemplation feels incredibly daunting to those of us who have built up images of the leaders presiding over our whole worlds. But it is crucial that we realize all this is okay. It is normal. We are allowed to reinvest in new directions and extend ourselves beyond our current definitions of who we are. At such times, we just need to ask for assistance, to pay more attention to our own needs and vision, to demand time to ourselves. When I finally did that, I realized that the world was changing, and I needed to change too. I realized I was spending an inordinate amount of energy trying to keep the world as it was, all on my own. That stubborn refusal to move with the world meant God was moving in one direction and I was moving in another. Or rather, I was staying put. He was calling out to me, and I was trying not to hear Him. It was only when I reached out to others to help me learn and share with me their understandings that I became empowered enough to feel the freedom to make new changes and to move in the direction He wanted me moving in the first place.

The key to all this is truth and the journey to truth, or as we have called it in this book, self-actualization. Remember, Jesus makes it real for us when he reminds us to know the truth and allow it to set us free. Truth cuts to the heart of how we feel about ourselves, our relationships, our work in the world, our God, and others; it reveals the person we know we ought to be deep down. It's a cure for what ails our souls, but we have to be willing to take it.

So many times, we try to hide our true selves from God and from our closest friends and family, because we are afraid to show our true selves to ourselves. What will people think of us if we actually ask for help? How low will they consider us if we go to them for support? These worries keep us trapped behind our curtain, afraid to even peek out and see if everyone is buying our sham. This isolation, even from ourselves, is not the happiness we pretend it is. It is a lonely kind of stress. What can really make us happy is being comfortable in our own skin. What really makes us feel good is being with people who genuinely care and are determined to stay and help us. There is a sense of well-being that comes from knowing we are capable and competent in what we do, and in admitting the limits of what that capability is. Moreover, knowing that God knows our true selves and loves our true selves—and that we are accepted for who we are in the company of those who acknowledge their own struggles—provides a sense of peace that sustains us even on the most perilous journey.

What can really make us happy is being comfortable in our own skin.

It is time to leave the fantasy world we have constructed behind in which we are everyone's superhero. We already know we cannot keep traveling at warp speed. Our engines are breaking down, and no one is going to do the repairs unless we call out for help. We need to recalibrate, take a breath, harmonize our different selves, reinvest in God, and extend into new challenges. And to do all that, we need to build a support team to keep those engines running. Because if they ever give out, we'll be no use to anyone. Struggling to be what we are

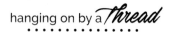

never going to be is not at all productive; tapping into who we are and nurturing what we find is going to pave the way for true fulfillment.

In life, we are going to experience more change and more transition than we could ever expect. Our list of responsibilities will always be growing longer. We cannot stop this, and we should not want to. Instead, we should be ready to embrace it. We can be ready to do the hard work to take ourselves to our own next level, but we aren't going to get there without a little help. The thread is often stronger than we could ever imagine, but it has to be reinforced by the love and understanding of friends, family, and God. The stress of life is God's way of bringing us to and through points of great change, but we are not meant to face change alone. David could not do it alone, nor Paul, nor any of the prophets. We have the tools of change at our disposal— the dreams, the desires, and the talent—but to really better our lives, we must learn to let God teach us how to use them and show us who is partnered with us for our success. Only then will be ready to face the new version of ourselves at the end of this journey, and to develop that person to be all we are capable of being.

The stress of life is God's way of bringing us to and through points of great change, but we are not meant to face change alone.

BREAKOUT SESSION WITH BISHOP THOMAS:

Hanging On By a Thread: The Power of Advice and Pilgrimage

What would you say is your greatest accomplishment in life personally? Professionally? Emotionally? Spiritually? Do you feel you accomplished this on your own or did you need help? If you say on your own, take a step back and look for those in the distance who supported you to your goal. Record your thoughts here:

_____

_____

_____

_____

_____

_____

_____

_____

_____

_____

_____

_____

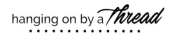

How would you tell another person how to help him or herself? What advice would you provide based on what you've read thus far in the book? What do you think will work or what has worked for you? Further, what are you going to try (that you read about here) that you would advocate for someone else to try?

_____

_____

_____

_____

_____

_____

_____

_____

_____

_____

_____

_____

What are your top five greatest goals in life? Think professionally, publicly, personally, and privately. What kind of support will you need to accomplish them?

_____

_____

_____

_____

_____

_____

_____

_____

_____

_____

_____

_____

_____

CHAPTER **NINE**

· ·

Discover and Develop You:
The New You at the End
of the Renewal Cycle

Now that we come to the final step of the THREAD Principle, I hope we are beginning to the see the fruits that are born from taking a breath, harmonizing our different selves, reinvesting in God, extending ourselves, and accepting advice. In the journey towards self-actualization, we have now learned to **strengthen the thread** instead of letting it fray away, and now all that is left is to discover the new you—the actualized you—and develop that you further.

Not that developing a new you is easy work. At this point, we understand that we have to accept change in our lives, but allowing that change to blossom and grow, allowing it to renew us, is no simple task. In truth, some of what makes us so successful is the fact that we have thrived in who we were before—who we have spent years presenting to the world. Finding a way to continue as leaders with a new focus can be intimidating. Those of us who strive for perfection tend to hole up and concentrate on a single area of our lives, building our careers and identities around a single "success measurement," which we continually work at refining at the expense of everything else. Now, as we step into our Fear Zones and accept the help of others to move into a new stage of life, we are afraid to break away from a self that has worked well for so long, stale or damaging as it is now. We spend so long laboring over a single part of our identity, we come to think it is the only thing that defines us. In reality, what defines us can be so much more.

> *At this point, we understand that we have to accept change in our lives, but allowing that change to blossom and grow, allowing it to renew us, is no simple task.*

In order to be more, though, we need to recognize when a chapter of our lives—or, in this case, a book—has come to an end. Consider the analogy, "seedtime and harvest, planting and reaping." In the all too familiar model, the seed dies to give birth to the plant. It is a means to an end—a death to beget a life. It is an easy analogy to use and understand, but it isn't necessarily easy to accept. Of course, we know that transition is never easy, that just because one stage ends and a new one begins doesn't mean we're ready for it. Change is uncertain, disconcerting, and yes, we can even say it's scary! The Fear Zone got its name for a reason. It's not easy to accept when our college days are over and responsibility and employment suddenly become necessary, or when our children leave home for lives of their own, leaving us with empty houses and empty hours. Hardest of all is the change demanded of us when a loved one passes. But change can still feel difficult even if it isn't always so dramatic or drastic. Just the simple transition of time is hard to come to terms with as we move from young adulthood into middle age, or middle age into retirement. In life, we constantly change and grow, and navigating that change carefully for a more contented and fulfilling life is the only pathway to happiness.

In his book, *Life Launch*, writer and expert in life-work balance and retirement, Frederic Hudson, tells us that change is not a single step, a course we take and graduate from, but part of a cycle that constantly leads us to grow and expand our sense of self. He says, "Life with its recurring seasons is a self-renewing process" *(Life Launch, pg. 53)*. He describes our journey in life as two separate ones—the "Outer Journey" and the "Inner Journey." He elaborates further:

> When you're in a transition, at first you feel out of sorts, but in time, you become renewed and self-sufficient. Because your interface with the world around you seems tentative, you invest most highly in the world within you. You seek to learn, discover, and grow as a person. This is your inner journey into your identity, self-esteem, and core values. In a transition, you concentrate on refurbishing your own inner self—the vital center of all renewal. You awaken to new forces and callings within yourself. You discover new possibilities for your life ahead.

As we come to a close in this book, it is important to recognize what Hudson is talking about. The THREAD Principle is, at its core, about renewal, about allowing us to "learn, discover, and grow." These transitional moments are scary to us at the time, but they lead to a life that is richer and more balanced. And as we graduate from the THREAD Principle, we have to recognize that the journey is not over. In fact, throughout our lives, we will find that we have to come back to the THREAD Principle as we continue to change and evolve in new directions.

As we cast our eye forward, we must consider what it is that intimidates us about this process. In part, what disturbs us so much is the deep confusion such moments cause. Every time we feel pressed to change, we are forced to tap directly into our most private selves, and we often do not like what we see or how the experience makes us feel. As we already know, it is in our private selves that we find our hidden away insecurities, the monsters we refuse to call ugly. But this process, though intimidating, is by no means negative. Thankfully, the voice of God is enough to get us moving in that right direction.

Unrest proved to be a good thing in my life. When I tapped into my insecurities and took the opportunity to move in a different direction through the THREAD Principle, I grew in many ways. Prayer took on new meaning. It became a necessity and not a luxury. I found myself before God seeking the understanding that seemed so impossible to find otherwise. I was tired of restlessness, and I knew God and God alone could walk me through the process. He, of course, did not let me down. Through His guidance, I took risks that I had never considered before. I charted new courses that took me well along the path to self-actualization, through my Fear Zone, through all my different lives and different selves, until I made decisions on my behalf that felt true to the me of today and not the me of decades before. Finally.

We all need this kind of ability to find renewal in our moments of crisis. For all of us, as we come out of that cycle of *"I'm working too hard, I'm not good enough, I'm at a loss regarding what to do"* and embrace our new selves, we need to keep the Hudson Institute's Renewal Cycle in mind. It is imperative that as we move beyond the THREAD Principle and get to know this new person we have become, that we recognize

The **Renewal Cycle**

the constant need to rejuvenate every now and then and continue to renew our *joie de vivre* (zest for life).

The Hudson Institute's Renewal Cycle entails four main stages:

1. Go for It!
2. Stuck in the Doldrums
3. Cocooning
4. Getting Ready for the Next Chapter

We are all familiar with the first stage. As leaders, we're all "Go for It" people; that's what has brought us to this moment of stress, success, and responsibility. It's also what has brought us to this moment of healing at the end of the THREAD Principle. We had to go for it just to open this book, just to take a breath. If there is an opportunity, we take it.

In time, however, we all know that reality catches up with our ambition. As we progress in life and the THREAD Principle grows dusty as we take on new challenges, we may begin to realize that everything is not quite as satisfying as we had hoped it would be. Life will continue to demand change and adaptation. The renewal cycle doesn't stop once we've come out of our current crisis. Perhaps the job we interview for doesn't actually come our way or the school that we so desperately want to get into just sent us a rejection letter. Or maybe we achieve our new goals, only to realize that our new job comes with more responsibility and less free time than what we have now, and paying for the advanced degree isn't as easy or straightforward as we dreamed. Even as THREAD draws us back to the person we are today, tomorrow we will again be someone else. Inevitably, we will again find that our lifestyles don't match our needs and we will find ourselves lost, once again, in the day-to-day routine of it all.

Life will continue to demand change and adaptation.

In that moment, we will find ourselves inhabiting the "Stuck in the Doldrums" phase. This phase can come unannounced and can stay for a long while. Until the THREAD Principle, many of you may have been stuck in this place for years. You know the story: as we settle into self-sacrificing routines, we settle into bad feelings about ourselves and about our decisions. We become firmly entrenched in our Comfort Zones. We become stagnant and reluctant to even contemplate the smallest changes in our lives. In this phase, taking risks and charting new courses would do wonders for our lives, and we have to remember to focus ourselves on branching out and pursuing new things, even when we are afraid to let go and start anew.

When you reenter this period, don't lose faith. There are steps that can be taken now to knock down the walls of these doldrums and move forward again in life. Despite the sense of helplessness in this moment, this is the time when we can seize initiative. If we return again to the THREAD Principle—repeat the steps and rediscover ourselves again—we can begin to prepare ourselves for the new changes ahead, entering the "Cocooning" stage where we can make progress in reestablishing our identity and then "Get Ready for the Next Chapter."

It's important to remember, as we draw to a close, that life's journey to self-actualization is continuous. There is no finish line. The cycle, as the term suggests, is a cycle (circle). While we have spent long periods of our lives—in my case nearly 41 years—slowly and imperceptibly sinking back and forth into our own personal doldrums, it does not mean we are impervious to falling back in now that we've learned to

stop **hanging on by a thread**. But now we know that life isn't hopeless in the doldrums; life is, in fact, waiting to burst forth again in exciting new directions. We just have to let it.

At some points in all of our journeys, we realize that we have to evolve. In my case, after nearly forty years, I knew that I had to go beyond the preacher that I was and explore the person beyond the profession. I wanted to work with leaders and individuals in a new way. I wanted to coach and consult. I wanted to help people grow in their skills and abilities and in their faith. I felt that there was more to me and my life. When I finally left the doldrums with the THREAD Principle and entered my "cocoon," I realized that I had more to offer, and there was more of me that needed to be explored. I discovered that God's plan for me was bigger than my view of His call upon my life. He had more in store for me. It was time for me to enter my "next chapter," which was to lead others to turn the page as well.

At some points in all of our journeys, we realize that we have to evolve.

Life is a process more than a single set task. As we make our way through, we begin to discover new capabilities and skills that God has honed in us. The revelation we come to in the "Cocooning" stage is that our understanding of who we are and what we are to do evolves over time. We are not meant to stay in the narrow areas where we are comfortable. And now that we are on the path to finding that next chapter, that next phase, we have to keep in mind that wherever we land next will not be the last chapter either. We only stay where we are because we are fearful: afraid of being hurt and vulnerable, and even worse, afraid of failure. Life is about discovery, about developing ourselves as we search to become self-actualized.

> *We only stay where we are because we are fearful: afraid of being hurt and vulnerable, and even worse, afraid of failure.*

The key is in understanding that one change is not the only change. The seasons and cycles in our lives will bring us around to a time of reflection and change again and again. The world would be a bland place if there were only ever one spring. Think of the wonder of contrast that comes with the snows of winter and the baking heat of summer, the first shoots of green in March or April and the range of colors come October. Nature displays all its beauty in its changing seasons, and we are meant to take our lesson from it. We, too, have much to give beyond the narrow purposes we assign ourselves in life in any one season.

New opportunities and relationships waiting in the wings are the things in life that will spark exploration of ourselves, our purpose, and our place with God. What makes the Discovery and Develop step of THREAD so difficult is a need to commit to no longer just making small changes, but allowing the change of life to reinvigorate and redirect us in large and surprising ways. In my case, I finally managed to emerge from my cocoon by developing my consulting skills and becoming a certified coach, which complements my role as pastor and fulfills a goal that developed over the years. When I did so, I found that my present (true) calling had been on the threshold for some time; I just had to go through the stages of change in order to get myself there.

With this book, I continue that journey, taking another step towards change, development, and personal truth. I no longer worry about whether others truly know me or I know myself; I know the answer. I know myself.

New opportunities and relationships waiting in the wings are the things in life that will spark exploration of ourselves, our purpose, and our place with God.

Variation and self-discovery are not things to shuffle off to the side; they are meant to be central to our journeys. Imagine all we would lose if the Bible were but a single book, just Genesis or the Gospel of John. Imagine all we would lose of the word of God. We, too, are tomes. And we must allow ourselves to discover our next chapters.

BREAKOUT SESSION WITH BISHOP THOMAS:

Hanging On By a Thread: The Renewal Cycle

How much time do you give to thinking about new possibilities in life? Maybe, on a smaller scale, you have always wanted to take a class, or on a larger scale, you have thought about changing careers or moving to a new location. Talk about those ideas here. What spurs you to action, and what prevents you from acting on these possibilities?

_____

_____

_____

_____

_____

_____

_____

_____

_____

_____

_____

_____

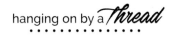

Detail some of your daily, weekly, or monthly routines here. Can you find patterns that are repetitive and don't make you happy? By contrast, can you find things that make you happy or that complete your sense of self or your sense of success for a given time period?

_____

_____

_____

_____

_____

_____

_____

_____

_____

_____

_____

_____

_____

How would you describe your "inner life" or your "inner journey?" Are there childhood dreams and goals that you never discuss? Are there new, adult goals that have changed since you got deeper into your career or family life? What steps would you take to make these goals happen and have these dreams realized?

_____

_____

_____

_____

_____

_____

_____

_____

_____

_____

_____

_____

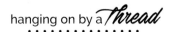
Talk here about how you might take the steps detailed in the Renewal Cycle in order to improve your life. How would you slow down? How would you get to know yourself? Further, how would you show yourself to the world? What do you need to do to transform yourself into a happier, healthier, more successful you?

_____

_____

_____

_____

_____

_____

_____

_____

_____

_____

_____

_____

CONCLUSION

· · · · · · · · · · · · · · · · · · · ·

Life as a Pilgrimage

In this book, I have tried to address some of the issues that have plagued all of us—saints, ain'ts, saviors, and normal Christians alike. I have tried to find the means to help those who decided along the way that they were too busy to help themselves. Like the quinine I already mentioned, however, this advice can be hard to take if we don't find the internal strength to hold our breath and take our medicine. Yet, we can find that strength—as all Christians have before us—if we just look at how the saints and disciples dealt with their own struggles and need for help. We, too, can strengthen the thread if we look first to strengthening our faith by engaging in honest dialogue with God. The stories of faith we read in the Bible and in the biographies of early martyrs and testifiers are stories of God intervening to restore hope and purpose. It is the testimony of the saints that should encourage us to believe that God will do the same for us. Their stories are a wake-up call; they awaken us to the depth of our pain but also to the grace that will restore us. I do believe that is one of the hallmarks of our faith. We come to understand the power of God is available to put us back together again, no matter how broken we feel in the moment. All we have to do is let Him. As David said, "He restores my soul." But like all of God's acts, He does not always restore us in the most direct ways. Rejuvenation and change require time, even with the THREAD Principle, and often, they require a sort of journey.

spoke at an interfaith gathering in Este, Japan. During my referred to the American author and philosopher Henry David ʒreau. Later in the day, a Hindu friend mentioned to me that he very much liked that reference and that it meant a lot to him. He had read a lot about the transcendental writers and knew that they were influenced heavily by some Eastern religions. He shared with me that he had gone to Walden Pond on one of his trips to America. He described it as feeling like he had been "on pilgrimage." For him, it was a spiritual, transformative experience, and he cherished the blessing it had been to him. I told him that pilgrimage is not a word we use much in our culture. In America, we wouldn't say we are going on a pilgrimage, we would say we are going on vacation (if we busy leaders even do that). We go see where *Dallas* was filmed or where Motown recorded. We go to visit monuments or museums or beaches, but we rarely look for spiritual growth or enlightenment on such trips. We don't turn our far too infrequent breaks into pilgrimages. And when we talk about pilgrims, we're thinking about Thanksgiving.

Yet, real pilgrimage is a powerful concept, even if our society has forgotten it. It offers us the opportunity to reconnect with the power and presence of God and creation and to rediscover ourselves. It is intentional, and it acknowledges our need for change and development that is guided by our spiritual connection with the almighty. Throughout this book, I have regularly referred to the THREAD Principle by the more common word in our language—journey—but THREAD is really a pilgrimage back to ourselves and back to our God. This is not a pilgrimage that has a definite final location or end date. We cannot complete the THREAD Principle and walk away. Instead, we have to constantly rededicate ourselves to this pilgrimage of self-discovery and self-actualization. We have to always make time for it in our lives.

CONCLUSION
· · · · · · · · · · · · · · ·

Eastern religions understand this and put more emphasis on the importance and act of journeying to rekindle the spiritual fire, and they are not alone. Our Christian faith teaches us that our Sunday experience ought to be seen as a pilgrimage, but that aspect of our worship is seldom highlighted. Instead, people see attending church as forced involvement, as a chore where it should be an act of faith and discovery. Our lack of actual pilgrimage and our spurning of metaphorical pilgrimage leaves us at a great disadvantage in our modern lives. Pilgrimage creates awe and wonder when we are stuck in mundanities, when we are stressed by all the tiny details that hold together all the complicated lives and selves we lead. Pilgrimage can help to establish for us the importance of our faith, the meaning of our definition of self, and the power of the connection we share with God.

I know the power of this firsthand. I remember my first trip to Bethlehem, standing in the Church of the Nativity, the purported birthplace of Jesus. I remember the feeling of awe and sense of wonder as I walked through the structure. Whether it is the place of the Savior's actual birth or not, I do not know, but what I know is that I felt a sense of connection, healing, and renewal. It was humbling and heartwarming. The act of pilgrimage is not about tourism. Instead, it is an ongoing movement toward God. It does require a journey for us, not just to Bethlehem or Walden Pond, but to ourselves. It is a spiritual motion, taking step after step toward God, trusting in His path for us. Making a pilgrimage implies reconnecting to the things in our lives that have meaning and importance or, in some cases, should have that honor. It implies inner renewal.

This is not always an easy process. Martin Luther famously climbed the Scala Sancta—the 28 steps that walked up to Pontius Pilate's praetorium relocated to Rome—on his knees. In the Middle Ages, people would travel across nations on foot just to reach a symbol that drew them closer to themselves and God. A pilgrimage is meant to be a rigorous journey which earns the truth that is present at the end. That is what the THREAD Principle is meant to offer us.

No matter how busy our professional, public, personal, and private lives are, we have to allow this sense of pilgrimage to enter our daily lives. We must be pilgrims in our every step, making discoveries about the relationship between our faith and our fulfillment. We have to be honest with ourselves and with God, even questioning our previous relationship with Him and our sense of faith, success, and happiness. Obviously, this can be somewhat out of our Comfort Zone, but as we've learned in this book, that is kind of the point.

This has been the path of every Christian before, and the people of God before that. Elijah made a pilgrimage to Horeb to get his questions answered by God. Jeremiah declared that he was done with faith then reaffirmed it, saying it was like *"a fire shut up in my bones"* (Jeremiah 20:19). Like the people before us, we have to admit the issues that are within us first, then wrestle with what they mean for our destiny. The only way we can resolve anything is to have serious heart-to-heart talks with God. Sometimes, we meet God while we are walking along the way. At other times, we hear God's voice in worship service. Still, at other times, we meet Him at the crossroads of indecision and our struggle. The point, though, is motion—step by careful step toward God in whatever place He chooses to seek us out. We *must* allow this sense of pilgrimage to inhabit us, and it *must* have all of our trust behind it. After all, the pilgrims of the past would travel countries and continents in the time before cars, planes, and trains. Even today, people of other faiths willingly cross the whole world. We, too, must develop this journeying mentality, even if we don't leave our homes.

Our quest is for deep and abiding spiritual honesty with ourselves and God, and it is not an idle quest. We need to understand that, through the years since Jesus walked the earth, successful men and women have been challenged by questions of faith and fulfillment, by a search for success and purpose. It would be great if our faith issues fit perfectly in a box with a bow, but we have to admit that we have some complicated feelings regarding what is expected of us. **Hanging on by a thin thread** never feels good, and as I've mentioned before in this book, it can even be dangerous.

We have to take authority and allow ourselves to ask the hard questions about our effectiveness, our success, and our happiness. That's not to say it is not also important to take the time to develop our career and our public image, but there is no substitute for the pilgrimage to self-discovery. The early Church Fathers stressed the discipline of solitude to make sure that time was always made for personal one-on-one time with God and the self. We may not choose their path, but I think it is important to find some space and time for this same process, and also to surround ourselves with people on a similar quest who are challenging themselves to find the same answers we are seeking. We may still falter or at times we may feel that we are going to fall off the rock of equilibrium, but by allowing the THREAD Principle to guide us back to getting to know ourselves, we can see positive change in our lives and develop the confidence to continually reassess and reaffirm our life with God. Through God, and through using the THREAD Principle, we will find our fulfillment and strength.

ABOUT THE
AUTHOR

• • • • • • • • • • • • • • • • • • • •

Dr. Walter S. Thomas, Sr.

Dr. Walter S. Thomas, Sr. has been Pastor of New Psalmist Baptist Church in Baltimore, Maryland, a large and expanding urban ministry, since 1975. There, he has developed innovative programs in Christian education, discipleship training, and Bible study. Under his leadership, the church has also started a national television broadcast of services called "Empowering Disciples," which is featured on the Word Network and on WJZ TV in Baltimore every Sunday.

As a popular and highly regarded Executive and Personal Coach with over 30 years of experience in the field, Dr. Thomas is in high demand to lead workshops and seminars across the country on building effective ministry teams and on preparing executives in all capacities and professions for next steps in leadership.

Dr. Thomas is also the Presiding Prelate of the Kingdom Association of Covenant Pastors, a fellowship of pastors committed to the call the Lord has placed on their lives and in endeavoring to encourage,

167

assist, edify, and celebrate one another in overcoming challenges and building God's Kingdom.

He holds a Bachelor of Science in Economics from the University of Maryland, a Master of Divinity from Howard University, a Doctor of Ministry from St. Mary's Seminary and University, and honorary Doctor of Divinity degrees from both Virginia Seminary and Bethune Cookman College. This is his fourth book. He is the author of *Spiritual Navigation for the 21st Century* and *Good Meat Makes its Own Gravy*, as well as editor of *Outstanding Black Sermons Vol 4*.

Dr. Thomas strives to bring warmth and palatable leadership strategies to his role as an Executive and Leadership Coach for his clients, and he ministers to his congregation and church leadership with relatable techniques and solutions, leading others to call him "The Pastor's Pastor." He lives with his wife and committed partner in ministry, Patricia, in Baltimore, Maryland. The couple has three grown children: Joi, Walter Jr., and Joshua.